SELF-
SUFFICIENCY

ON A SHOESTRING!

SELF-SUFFICIENCY

ON A SHOESTRING!

Recipes for a new, fun and free lifestyle

ALAN & GILL BRIDGEWATER

FINE FOLIO
PUBLISHING

First published in the UK in 2012 by
Fine Folio Publishing Limited
6 Bourne Terrace, Bourne Hill, Wherstead,
Ipswich, Suffolk, IP2 8NG, UK
www.finefoliopublishing.com

ISBN 978-0-9570969-2-9

1 3 5 7 9 10 8 6 4 2

PRODUCED BY
Fine Folio Publishing Limited

DESIGNER
Glyn Bridgewater

ILLUSTRATOR
Gill Bridgewater

EDITOR
Alison Copland

Printed and bound by
Voion Printing Group (International) Co., Ltd
Unit 305–306, 3rd Floor, Yen Sheng Centre,
64 Hoi Yuen Road, Kwun Tong, KLN, Hong Kong

CONTENTS

HOWEVER MEAN YOUR LIFE IS, MEET IT:
DO NOT SHUN IT AND CALL IT HARD
NAMES. CULTIVATE POVERTY LIKE A
GARDEN... DO NOT TROUBLE YOURSELF TO
GET NEW THINGS... SELL YOUR CLOTHES
AND KEEP YOUR THOUGHTS.

WALDEN, HENRY DAVID THOREAU (1817–1862)
THOREAU'S ACCOUNT OF HIS EXPERIMENT IN SHOESTRING LIVING

INTRODUCTION

When Gill and I look around us, we see that most people are literally working themselves to death so that they can purchase yet more meaningless possessions, and in so doing they are trashing nature from all sides. Our way of tackling this sorry, potentially catastrophic state of affairs is not to try to change the world around us or to compete, but rather to modify the way we live. For us, being self-sufficient on a shoestring – always working to recycle and salvage – is not a chore but a challenge.

Our particular brand of self-sufficiency – we call it make-do-and-mend shoestring – draws its inspiration from our student days in the mid-1960s when the various modern back-to-the-land homesteading movements were beginning to take off. With their roots in the 1950s beatnik culture, and still further back in the William Morris medievalism movement that yearned to return to some sort of hands-on, rural-craftsmen past that believed that 'simplicity of life, even the barest, is not misery, but the very foundation of refinement', the main push of the 1960s self-sufficient good-life homesteaders was their alternative, counterculture lifestyle. The wonderful thing about these people was the way they recognized that, while living their city or suburban lives, they completely lacked any familiarity with such basics of life as food sources. Where do eggs and milk come from? How does a tree become a table? How does corn become bread? They felt out of touch with nature.

In much the same way as our grandparents had no choice, during and after the Second World War, other than to build their world afresh using a mix of salvaged materials and whatever natural materials they could find, Gill and I have created our own self-sufficient world using a mix of natural materials and recycled waste. Many of the things in and around our home – our clothes, the fabric of the house, our sheds and shelters, our tools and materials, all our garden carts and trucks – are either salvaged or made from a mix of salvaged and recycled component parts.

If you think that this way of life is all about cheap scrounging, you could not be more wrong. Shoestring self-sufficiency is about looking at your life afresh. For example, if some item in our home breaks or needs building – a coat hook, a shed, a table, a chair, a lamp – our first response is not to dip into our hard-earned money and buy a new product, but to look around and see if we can rework or make use of an existing item or material. Much the same goes for what we eat, how we heat the home, our transport and everything else – we always draw inspiration from our make-do-and-mend past.

Shoestring self-sufficiency is all win-win. Your hard-earned money stays in your pocket, you are recycling something that would otherwise go to waste, and best of all you get to experience the exciting, therapeutic, hands-on, skill-stretching challenge of creating something that, but for your resourceful input, would not exist. If you want to save money, have a life-long adventure and enjoy a whole heap of fun along the way, then just keep reading this book.

> **IF A MAN LOSES PACE WITH HIS COMPANIONS, PERHAPS IT IS BECAUSE HE HEARS A DIFFERENT DRUMMER. LET HIM STEP TO THE MUSIC WHICH HE HEARS, HOWEVER MEASURED, OR FAR AWAY.**
>
> *WALDEN*

DISCUSSION POINTS

VARIETIES OF SUSTAINABLE LIVING

A question we are often asked is: what does 'shoestring self-sufficiency' really mean? If we stay with the dictionary definition that says that the term 'self-sufficiency' is usually applied to some sort of personal or collective, sustainable, self-contained, or self-reliant way of living, then it follows that shoestring self-sufficiency is much the same – it is still about sustainable self-reliance – but it is further defined as being self-reliance with a one-eye-on-the-budget twist. If this definition makes you think that shoestring self-sufficiency is in some way about a mean-minded, penny-pinching, cold, and cheerless lifestyle – a sort of Scrooge-inspired way of living – then think again. Shoestring self-sufficiency is about looking at the way we are – what we eat, our clothing, our housing, our transport, the way we keep warm – and then, by means of a bit of joyous, brain-stretching lateral thinking, coming up with solutions that solve the problems without spending money.

Although shoestring self-sufficiency does in part draw inspiration from the homesteaders, survivalists, hippies, and various other back-to-the-land movements, we see it, primarily, as drawing inspiration from the 1940s wartime 'Dig for Victory' and 'Make-do-and-mend' movements. We are not suggesting that you slip into some sort of 1940s black-and-white time warp when the 'make-do-and-mend' philosophy permeated every aspect of British and American life, but rather we are saying that you could radically change your life by making objects and systems last longer, by not buying new, by growing and storing your own food, and by generally being thrifty. As we see it, and as we advocate in this book, there is challenging joy to be had from darning a sock, making jam, winemaking, foraging and such like. As my old grandpa used to say, 'There is no shame in mending an axe handle and sewing on a button – we need, for our own self-worth, to get back to the way it was.'

Our aim in writing this book is not to lecture, preach, or in any way moralize, but simply to share with you some of the financial and therapeutic pleasures of shoestring living.

City community projects, community gardens, and allotments

In the US, community gardens or Victory Gardens sprang up in the Second World War; however, the sizes vary hugely, with some gardens no larger than 5 ft (1.5 m) square. Allotments in the UK started in and around the early 1800s when small areas of land were spared from the Enclosure Acts and reserved for the poor. They range from 40 to 300 m² (430–3,250 sq. ft) per person, require membership and a very modest annual payment to the landowner; there is usually a waiting list of a year or more. In the UK, local authorities have a statutory duty to provide sufficient allotments if there is a demand. The produce is intended for consumption by the plot-holder and their family, as opposed to selling the produce. In Germany, growing vegetables and fruit on more than 1.4 million allotments was an essential part-time job during both wars, but nowadays these pastimes are enjoyed for the same reasons as elsewhere.

Guerrilla gardening

Planting vegetables on another person's unused land – usually in the city – without their permission was popularized by the Green Guerrilla group in New York in the 1970s. The secret, or sometimes highly visible, planting of fruit trees and edible perennials along riverbanks, ditches, and disused and derelict land continues today. In Parliament Square in London on May Day 2000, thousands of guerrilla gardeners planted vegetables and flowers and hung banners announcing 'Capitalism is Pants,' 'Resistance is Fertile,' and 'The Earth is a Common Treasury for All.' Direct action in Manchester, England, resulted in 'Leaf Street' – a community garden that was previously an urban street.

Urban foraging and dumpster diving (skipping)

It used to be that people who resorted to dumpster diving were forced to do so out of necessity, but today in Canada, for example, bottle collectors search garbage and dumpsters for recyclable materials and earn on average $40 per day. The other side to skipping is making use of the large amounts of food thrown away by supermarkets. This can be near its 'use by' date or just removed from the shelves to make room for new stock, but obviously comes with health risks, not least food poisoning! Foraging for nuts and berries and other plant food in the city on the roadside and in parks is common practice, but it is sometimes claimed that some plants absorb toxins from soil. Sound facts are difficult to come by, but it is obviously a good idea to avoid eating plants that are near to very busy roads where there might be high levels of lead, mercury, and asbestos.

Urban and semi-rural smallholding/ urban homesteading/backyard farming

This involves growing all you can and perhaps keeping some chickens and bees on a small patch of ground in an urban area. As a guide, the Dervaes family (owners of urbanhomestead.org) who live in Pasadena, California, and controversially registered 'urban homesteading' and 'urban homestead' as trademarks in 2010, produce 'over 6000 pounds of organic food annually on 1/10 of an acre.' An impressive achievement! Local urban homesteading events or farmer's markets are a good place to learn and swap information and possibly trade in goods (check first). Apart from the usual produce, such as pies, cakes, jam, and honey, you might get to see how a pig is butchered, and how sausages are made. See page 44 for more on urban self-sufficiency.

Simple living

This is all about simplifying your lifestyle. All you do is look at what you have and then cut and slash. For example, who needs a television, more than one light per room, a car, dozens of pairs of shoes, cakes, cookies, canned drinks, shop-bought sandwiches, body washes, shampoos, or new clothes for every season?

Smallholding/homestead/farmstead

In the US, a homestead is technically an area covering 65 hectares (160 acres), although the term is now used loosely to refer to a space big enough to be almost self-sustaining. A smallholding in the UK is meant to indicate a small farm, or as they say in Australia a 'hobby farm,' and can be as small as 2 hectares (5 acres). In New Zealand, 'lifestyle block' is another term for a smallholding.

Self-sufficient communities/ecovillages/communes

These are small groups of like-minded people who have usually voluntarily opted to lead an alternative, low-impact, stress-free lifestyle. This often involves camping in tents or building shacks, mud houses or yurts, sometimes squatting, sometimes living and working legally in woodland, for example. An important factor is sharing all aspects of life, including material goods and sometimes work and income, and everybody being considered equal. Some are centered around a religion.

Off-grid/autonomous sustainable house

At one time all houses were off-grid, but the modern versions may use sustainable building materials, are engineered to be cool in summer and warm in winter, and make use of all available high-tech equipment, generate renewable energy, and collect and recycle water. Some even feed energy into the grid. See page 52 for more on off-grid houses.

Wilderness/cabin living

If you have a mind to, you can live in the wilderness. All you do is pick a country – such as the US, Canada, or Australia – and then simply wander off into the woods with a tent and a backpack and set up home. Of course it is dangerous, and there are risks, but if it is excitement and low-cost living you want then it is an option.

Free land on offer in the US (schemes)

It seems unlikely, but there are places in the US where you can get land for free – in Kansas, Dakota, Alaska, and many other areas. For example, in Ellsworth County there are currently 23 lots available, and families with children stand to receive a money grant.

Free property to be found in the UK (unregistered)

Research suggests that about 40% of the land in the UK is unregistered. If you can find a piece of unclaimed land, and then occupy the land for 12 years without your claim being challenged, then it is yours.

Low-cost land and property overseas or in developing countries

There is low-cost land to be found in Spain, rural France, America, Canada, and many other countries. If you are keen, pick a country and then start researching the options. For example, I have just keyed 'low cost land in Northern Ontario' into an internet search engine, and 'a 40 acre wilderness plot at $13000', has popped up. The place has forest, water, and game such as moose and waterfowl.

Houseboats and seasteading

Permanent dwellings at sea are rare, but not unheard of. The intention of seasteading is to find an area of sea 370 km (200 nautical miles) away from land, live there freely in a self-sustaining way, and by definition be outside the law. Less dramatic and perhaps more attractive versions are living on a boat for long periods of time without staying longer than a visitor may stay in each harbor, or living on an operational or stationary houseboat or narrow boat. Over 15,000 people live on houseboats in the UK and the trend is on the rise in the US. Houseboats and floating homes or 'amphibious houses' in the US and Europe have not escaped land taxes or permission/zoning laws, but they benefit from utilities if you choose to have them and they certainly present an attractive option for living on a shoestring, especially if you combine this with an allotment or community garden.

House trailers/mobile homes, travel trailers/caravans, and RVs/camper vans

French circus performers as far back as 1800 lived in large wagons that incorporated a living space, and in the second half of the 19th century British Romani people (Gypsies) used smaller 'vardos' ('vardo' comes from the Iranian *vurdon* meaning cart). These horse-drawn homes were beautifully constructed and decorated with ornate carving and bright colors. By the 1920s, and along with a decline in horse-trading and crafts, the Romani travelers struggled to maintain their way of life. Modern caravans have largely replaced the folksy, hand-crafted versions and are more comfortable.

> NELL VENTURED TO STEAL A LOOK ROUND THE CARAVAN AND OBSERVE IT MORE CLOSELY... A SLEEPING-PLACE, CONSTRUCTED AFTER THE FASHION OF A BERTH ON BOARD SHIP, WHICH WAS SHADED, LIKE THE LITTLE WINDOWS, WITH FAIR WHITE CURTAINS, AND LOOKED COMFORTABLE ENOUGH... THE OTHER HALF SERVED FOR A KITCHEN, AND WAS FITTED UP WITH A STOVE WHOSE SMALL CHIMNEY PASSED THROUGH THE ROOF. IT HELD ALSO A CLOSET OR LARDER, SEVERAL CHESTS, A GREAT PITCHER OF WATER, AND A FEW COOKING-UTENSILS AND ARTICLES OF CROCKERY.
>
> *THE OLD CURIOSITY SHOP*, CHARLES DICKENS

The recent economic downturn has resulted in many people losing their jobs and their traditional homes, and many becoming homeless. Some live in tents, and others in vans and RVs/camper vans. Most are thoroughly depressed about the situation, but a few are finding the enforced simplification and downsizing to be liberating. One man who lives all year in a van has documented his progress on the internet and highlights benefits such as a low cost of living, new scenery, and following the warmer weather. There are severe problems with this lifestyle, of course, and the most obvious one is no access to utilities. Tax collected based on property value helps support communities, so locals may be hostile towards travelers for that reason, or they may worry about an increase in crime or camps becoming permanent and affecting the value of their properties.

Small/tiny house movement

In the US, the idea of building your own attractive and super-compact house became popular with the Tiny (Small) House Movement initiated by architect Sarah Susanka when she published her book *The Not So Big House* in 1997. The idea is to construct and live in a small house (no more than 46 m² /500 sq. ft) in order to reduce bills and environmental impact to a minimum, and also to simplify and declutter the home with the aim of freeing up people's time in order to focus on aspects of their lives other than earning money and housework. Small houses present problems when they clash with local building codes and neighbors who worry that they might devalue the houses in the area or lead to their own taxes increasing.

Often cities base their tax system on a minimum of 500 sq. ft to ensure adequate revenue, and this is an obstacle to getting zoning/planning permission. Also, because the small homes are cheap to build and maintain they have often been constructed as second homes; therefore the positive environmental aspect of their design comes into question. Others argue, however, that every small house is potentially a permanent residence.

Extreme downsizing and 'simplifying' is an upward trend in the US. Tiny homes are everywhere from Texas to Wisconsin. Beautifully designed eco-friendly DIY tiny homes, some built on trailers for the purpose of relocating in the near future or coming under the definition of temporary or mobile accommodation, and around 8 m² (85 sq. ft) in size, are on the increase. Typically the sleeping area is in the loft. Powered by propane for a heater, a gas ring for cooking, and solar energy for lighting and small electricals, and with a composting toilet, many also have showers included. Some get over the lack of washing facilities by coming to an arrangement with a neighbor (swap some work for use of their shower, for example). Most tiny houses sit in a friend's backyard. With no mortgage, there may also be no rent as long as the friend is happy with some gardening or cleaning in return. It is different from living in an aluminum or fiberglass trailer/mobile home, because it can be a lot cheaper, but it is also a chance to stamp your individuality on your home.

The Small House Society provide links to builders in the US who specialize in tiny houses, and over the last three years uptake has increased dramatically. If you are good at carpentry, or have friends that can teach you how, blueprints for doing it yourself can be found on the internet. Use salvaged 'vintage' timber and do not be afraid to adapt the design to suit free, low-cost, 'second-grade' or 'reject' insulation, windows, and other materials. Second-grade insulation can be half the price with no loss of efficiency if you use it correctly. Double-glazed windows rejected from jobs due to a mistake in dimensions can be one-fifth of the normal price. A single person with no building experience might attend a tiny house construction workshop and take three months to build a house, or it can be a three-week job for a skilled carpenter.

You will miss having a house as an asset, but the trade-off is that you will have more time and money... and prepare to leave most of your stuff behind!

ARRANGEMENTS AND SPECIAL EXCEPTIONS

Zoning laws/planning permission, building codes/regulations, permits, property taxes, and hostility from the local neighborhood are important issues to consider when attempting to live an alternative lifestyle in an unusual home, and especially if you are living 'on the road' or parked up somewhere in a caravan, tiny house on wheels, or other home that the authorities must define as 'temporary accommodation' for the purpose of controlling development and collecting tax. There are plenty of instances where a person or family can live very cheaply or more or less freely as long as they are on private land. For example, a person could rent a single room but have an allotment. A family might look after a fantastic house and plot of land for a wealthy owner and get paid and eat as many homegrown vegetables as they like. You might pitch a caravan on agricultural land or woodland for the purposes of working the land, and by special exception or by default you may eventually receive permission to live there permanently. Or a landowner may obtain permission through special exception for a tiny house to be permanently sited in their back yard. But do consider the following points.

* Homeowner associations may object even if your house is legal and make life unpleasant in an attempt to oust you.

* Trailers or non-permanent structures are not houses and are not affected by building codes (building regulations) but are regulated with the intention of restricting their location to trailer parks.

* 'Non-permanent structures' where they are allowed are often limited to say 90 days.

* Re-zoning an area is virtually impossible in residential areas and unlikely – although not impossible – in rural areas.

* Parking in a back yard with the owner's permission is a great option, but to be legal the property has to be re-zoned to a multi-family or multi-residence zone, which is rare but possible under special circumstances that are not defined; therefore you must be ready to put forward a very strong case and prepare for a long battle, which is likely to end in disappointment.

* Any attempt to live permanently in a temporary structure, even hidden away in a rural area, is likely to be identified quickly now that authorities have easy access to aerial photographs on the internet.

* Campgrounds/camping sites may not accept tiny houses on the basis that their appearance does not fit into people's perception of camping.

* Trailer/mobile home parks may also reject tiny houses because they fail to meet minimum standards, and because they do not know how to tax the home.

* If you are making a living from a woodland that you rent or own and can justify living there all the time – for example, you must be there round the clock for a good reason – the planning authority may allow development.

THE RECESSION

We all know about recession – it is a time when living costs rise and job prospects and salaries fall. That said, recession is also, perhaps more than anything else, a time of change and challenge, a time of opportunity rather than fear. Gill and I know about recession. We were not long married, and one day we were in work and the next – without much warning – we were out of a job with a minute income and little savings. We were fortunate in that we had grandparents who, because they had lived through one or two wars and a string of recessions, knew the way forward and were able to give advice. They knew about hunger, deprivation, war, recession, homelessness, the blitz, bad health, and so on. Their advice was as follows.

∗ When recession hits, greed is out and communities are in.

∗ Face up to the fact that things like new clothes, televisions, expensive holidays, eating out, and cars are all empty dross.

∗ If you truly cannot survive without things like fast food and high fashion, then you deserve to go down.

∗ Be positive and open-minded.

∗ Don't waste energy complaining about the way it was.

* Look at your skills and qualities.

* Look at your spending and make cuts – if you don't need it, then don't get it.

* Reduce your debts.

* Look at who, what, and where you are.

* Think small and tight, but at the same time be open to every opportunity that comes your way.

* Be ready to take a job at a lower salary.

* Be ready to move house and home.

The good news is that when Gill and I looked afresh at who and where we were, we gradually realized that there were new opportunities all around us. In fact, the moment we followed through on an opportunity that had been staring us in the face right through our difficulties it all came good. We moved house, stopped bemoaning our loss, started writing and illustrating, and here we are.

SAVING THE PLANET

We all know about global warming, the rise in average temperature of Earth's atmosphere and oceans, greenhouse gases gradually warming us up by effectively bouncing back and recycling some of the heat (thermal radiation) emitted by Earth, sea-level rises, the amount and pattern of rainfall changes, subtropical deserts expanding, glaciers, permafrost and sea ice diminishing, food shortages, heatwaves, extinctions – our planet is truly in a terrible state. So what can we do about it?

> **THANK GOD MEN CANNOT
> FLY AND LAY WASTE THE SKY
> AS WELL AS THE EARTH.**
> **HENRY DAVID THOREAU**

We could all sit back and 'fiddle while Rome burns' – that is what civilizations have done in the past and will no doubt do in the future (if we have a future) – but it is better if we as individuals don't worry so much about the big picture, but rather spend time and effort tidying up our own little mess. This is where shoestring self-sufficiency comes in. Changing to new low-energy light bulbs, darning our socks, recycling, eating less, keeping chickens, growing vegetables, cutting car use, and all the other good-life solutions are each small and somewhat laughable in themselves – what could be sillier than thinking we can save the planet by darning socks? – but if we all did our little bit then imagine how wonderful it could be.

Some encouraging facts

∗ Wind power generation worldwide is growing at the rate of 30% annually.

∗ PV (photovoltaic/solar cell) power stations are popular in Germany and Spain.

∗ The Geysers geothermal power installation in California has a rated capacity of 750 MW.

∗ Brazil has possibly the largest renewable energy program in the world.

∗ Ethanol fuel is widely available in the US.

∗ Renewable technologies are suited to remote areas.

∗ As of 2011, small-scale PV systems provide electricity to a few million households.

∗ Small-grid micro-hydro generators serve even more households.

∗ 50 million households use biogas from household digesters for cooking or lighting.

The International Energy Agency projected in 2011 that solar power generators may produce most of the world's electricity within 50 years. There are perceived shortages in the rare materials for making solar cells, but alternative materials have been proposed and the rare materials are now not as rare as we thought. Best of all, Ban Ki-moon, the United Nation's Secretary-General, thinks that renewable energy may substantially increase the prosperity of developing nations.

THIS IS THE WAY THE WORLD ENDS
THIS IS THE WAY THE WORLD ENDS
THIS IS THE WAY THE WORLD ENDS
NOT WITH A BANG BUT A WHIMPER.
THE HOLLOW MEN, T S ELIOT

FOOD

In developed countries we enjoy the sight of large, 'perfect' fruits and vegetables and neatly trimmed fat-free joints of meat, processed foods with soft textures, oily and sweet foods, fast foods and genetically modified (GM) foods (they don't always taste great!). Prices are going up all the time, but still represent the smaller part of our weekly expense. We know that there are chemicals in our food that should not be there and are the result of intensive farming, and the long-term consequences of eating GM food are not known, but generally we think we will probably survive eating the chemicals because humans are resilient. On top of that, we eat much more food than we should because it is so cheap, or perhaps because life is making us miserable. But intensive farming also has another price. It pollutes the environment and changes landscapes, and some pollution is not always obvious. For example, antifungal sprays used on Californian vineyards are the likely cause of an increase in natural levels of methyl mercury known to cause developmental defects.

In contrast, and for various reasons, developing countries do not have enough food. Global warming may be the cause of droughts, for example, but civil war, dictatorships, debts owed to developed countries, and huge fluctuations in world food prices are to blame. In 2010 the Food and Agriculture Organization of the United Nations (FAO) launched a worldwide campaign entitled 'The 1billionhungry Project', encouraging people 'to get angry at the fact that around a billion people suffer from hunger' – 14% of the world's population. Free or subsidized fertilizers and seeds have improved the situation in the short term by increasing harvests and bringing down food prices.

FOR MILLIONS OF PEOPLE IN DEVELOPING COUNTRIES, EATING THE MINIMUM AMOUNT OF FOOD EVERY DAY TO LIVE AN ACTIVE AND HEALTHY LIFE IS A DISTANT DREAM... THE STRUCTURAL PROBLEMS OF HUNGER, LIKE THE LACK OF ACCESS TO LAND, CREDIT AND EMPLOYMENT, COMBINED WITH HIGH FOOD PRICES REMAIN A DIRE REALITY.

FAO'S HAFEZ GHANEM

Interestingly, scientists have recently discovered that our early hunter-gatherer ancestors were not only able to forage and hunt for food and provide themselves with enough to keep them well nourished, but that the early self-sufficient farmers, by contrast, were not able to achieve the same level of nutrition. When land was partitioned and hunting and foraging were renamed poaching and trespassing, there were food shortages and malnutrition. So much for progress.

On the positive side, a healthy balance is often achieved today in self-sufficient farming communities in developing countries – there are no homeless or hungry, the physical exercise involved in planting, transplanting, harvesting, milling, hunting, and foraging keeps people fit, and there is enough organic food to keep them healthy. You might assume they work all day long to grow all that food, but in fact they work a small fraction of the time, enjoy numerous festivals, and have plenty of time to stand and stare and contemplate what it means to be alive.

The way it was

When Gill and I listen to young people, we hear that for the most part they think that any time before the 1960s was a black-and-white time of want and need. However, as far as food was concerned it was, in many ways, a time of small and beautiful. We did not have shop-bought cakes and cookies, unlimited amounts of meat, yogurt, olive oil, pasta, curries, takeaways, chocolate-covered breakfast cereal, and all the other snacks, but what we did have was good, clean, honest, and above all chemical free.

When Gill and I are in the garden bringing in the harvest, in the kitchen cooking and storing away our produce, and at the table eating, I see in my mind's eye...

The old brew-house was full of logs of wood, piled high against the walls... on the kitchen walls hung the sides of bacon and from the hooks in the ceiling dangled great hams and shoulders. Bunches of onions were twisted in the pantry... The floor of the chamber was covered with apples, rosy red apples, little yellow ones, like cowslip balls, wizenedy apples with withered wrinkled cheeks... Stone jars like those in which the forty thieves hid stood on the pantry floor, filled with white lard, and balls of fat tied up in bladders hung from hooks. Along the broad shelves round the walls were pots of jam, blackberry and apple, from the woods and orchards. Victoria plum... black currant. Pickles and spices filled old brown pots... under the stairs were bottles of elderberry wine, purple, thick, and sweet... hot ginger.

THE COUNTRY CHILD, ALISON UTTLEY, 1931

QUALITY OF LIFE

Every day of our self-sufficiency-on-a-shoestring lifestyle is an adventure. We grow fruit and vegetables in a no-dig raised bed vegetable garden, we store our produce or give it to friends and neighbors, our geese give us eggs, our bees give us a huge amount of pleasure and of course honey that we eat and sell, we have a log-burning stove that has introduced us to the ecologically sound craft of coppicing, we have fitted solar water heaters and solar voltaic electricity generators, we have refurbished an old tractor... and I could continue. For us, the biggest joy of shoestring self-sufficiency is that we can, to a great extent, shape our lives to suit our own fears, strengths, pleasures, and weaknesses. Imagine no more kowtowing to some sort of relentless money-making, life-squeezing company, no more long hours spent commuting to work, no more 'pulling together' for some sort of 'phony' company cause. Life is very good. Are you ready for it?

If, however, you think that our brand of self-sufficiency can only be worked from the plush comfort of a money-padded country cottage, then think again. We know a young couple who moved from a big city to a mobile-home-type property on the outskirts where the enclosed garden was covered by concrete and corrugated-iron chicken sheds. Undaunted, they recycled the iron sheds to make raised beds, set these on the concrete slabs, and filled them up with the chicken manure. Now, they have a vegetable garden, chickens, and bees, and they have planning permission to build a small single-story eco-home. Everyone is happy, including the local council and the neighbors.

ADVENTURE

YOUR OPTIONS

Our big shoestring self-sufficiency adventure

Way back in the late 1950s, about ten or so years after the war, times were very hard; there was not much money and just about everything – food, clothing, and manufactured goods – was in desperately short supply. Little wonder that when I was a kid playing out my childhood fantasies in and around my granny's isolated country cottage – building camps and shelters, digging holes, keeping chickens, and making my own tools, toys, and contraptions – just about every aspect of my life, and of all the lives of our friends and neighbors, was dominated by the need to think 'shoestring' or 'make-do-and-mend.' If I wanted materials like rope, string, leather, canvas, elastic, and wood, or items like wheels, springs, nails, screws, and bolts, then I had to recycle, salvage, or swap. If a tool or material was not to be obtained for free or for trade, it was not obtained at all.

In this environment, packing cases became dens and wood to be worked, old prams and bicycles and all the associated nuts, bolts, and bits and bobs became go-karts and garden trucks – everything from the last bent nail through to lengths of wire was recycled. So, for example, when I wanted a tent, I made it from an ex-military canvas tarpaulin, and when I wanted to extend the life of my school sandals – so that they would take me through the summer holidays – I cut off the toes and worked them so that they became moccasins. When an item around the house broke – a bit of furniture, a door catch, a switch – then between us we simply set to and made a repair. Even in the good times we grew most of our food and made lots of our clothes – that is just the way it was.

Much the same story applies to Gill, who spent her childhood living in a corrugated tin shack, so she also had no choice but to be self-reliant and self-contained. I am pretty sure I have said it already, but it is not at all surprising that when Gill and I met in the early 1960s our idea of heaven on earth was to live deep in the country in an isolated ruin of a farmhouse with no running water and no electricity. As for our self-sufficiency plans at that time, they were pleasingly uncomplicated and direct – we would rebuild the house, set the barn up as a pottery and weaving workshop, and generally establish our own neat slice of shoestring pioneer paradise.

So here we are at this end of the great adventure living in a small wooden shack of a house set in 1.5 hectares (4 acres) of field and woodland, and still happily doing our best to be self-sufficient. Yet, of course, as many of our stressed-out, slaving 9-to-5, big-earning, fair-weather 'friends' delight in telling us, we are not totally, absolutely, completely self-sufficient – how could we ever be? – because we also earn money writing about our various garden, craft, and eco activities. However, we have a flock of geese, five hives of bees, a beautiful orchard, and a very fruitful raised bed no-dig vegetable garden. Our little wooden cottage is massively insulated, there is a passive solarium along the sunny side, a wood-fired stove chugs away through the winter, there is a huge solar water heater on the roof, and we are just about to fit a bank of photovoltaic panels to provide some of our electricity. Our energy bills are bucking the trend by going down. Even better, we are happily swapping, gifting, and trading with a group of like-minded friends. It is a challenge, but on the plus side our shoestring lifestyle saves us huge amounts of money, most of our food is organic, and best of all, no doubt because it reminds us of our childhood, our way of living is just plain old-fashioned fun.

Thinking through your adventure

The very fact that you are reading these words suggests that you are playing around with the notion of shoestring self-sufficiency. Good – now for the important questions that you must answer before you set out on your great adventure.

Questions to ask yourself

Are you going to stay put in your home and aim for self-sufficiency as is, or do you need to move? Can you somehow cut your costs to the bone by moving to a different country? Are you going to continue in full-time work? Do you have enough money to make it happen? Are you no more than a dreamer who enjoys the dream, or are you really going to make it happen? Are you ready and willing to drop some of the dross of modern living – designer labels, everything new, eating foreign imported food, and all the other expensive and unnecessary frills? Do you think that you and yours – your friends, partner, kids – are all going to enjoy the adventure?

URBAN SELF-SUFFICIENCY

Is it possible to become shoestring self-sufficient in town? While the answer has to be yes – you can join an allotment society, you can join an inner-city community project, you can grow food on flat roofs and in pots and containers, and you can keep chickens and generally green up your life – I would always counter with the question why would you choose this difficult way forward when it is so much easier to move to the country where land is readily available, property renting prices are lower, and the quality of life is so much higher? Nevertheless, if you really do want to go for the urban option, then you need to search out like-minded individuals and groups and see what they advise. The really good news if you like the notion of small-town self-sufficiency is that (at the time of writing) on www.organic-gardening-and-homesteading.com/homesteading_today. html there are towns in the rural Midwest of the US that are looking for residents and will give you free land if you are willing to move there.

Large garden options

If you have a large garden of 280–370 m² (3,000–4,000 sq. ft) and if you are willing to turn more or less all of the space over to food production – vegetables, chickens, eggs, and perhaps bees – there is no reason why you should not grow most of your own food. We have an elderly friend who grows all her own vegetables, has fruit trees, and keeps bees – she feeds herself and her husband and sells surplus honey at the gate.

The upside of urban shoestring

I don't understand it myself, but research suggests that some people are attracted by the buzz of living in the heart of a busy town/city community – they find the noise and the hum inspirational. If your notion of shoestring self-sufficiency has more to do with make-do-and-mend and salvaging basic materials than growing food, then perhaps urban living is a good way forward. Allotments and some city community projects are subsidized – a very good option if you like the notion of working in a group. If your idea of shoestring involves cutting costs by buying time-dated food and selling and trading at markets – a sort of modern urban survivalism – then urban living might also be a good choice for you.

The downside of urban shoestring

Although you can grow food like herbs and salad crops in a window box or in pots on the patio, for example, we are only talking small. Urban living is always going to be restricted; there are more rules and codes and lots of people to object to your activities. In many countries – such as the US and the UK – there are numerous town/city codes that ban the keeping of livestock such as pigs, chickens, and bees. Experience tells us that keeping chickens and having an allotment in town is a really bad idea; vegetable crops get vandalized and chickens get stolen – sad, but true.

TOWN AND VILLAGE
SELF-SUFFICIENCY

In the context of this book, a village-type set-up might be anything from a tiny tight-knit community in an English shire through to a small but sprawling community in say France, Germany, or the American Mid-West. The basic scenario is that the community is small – no more than 3,000–4,000 people – with houses that range from large and wealthy through to humble, with most houses having good-sized gardens. If you like small rural communities and lots of fields, farms, woods, and water, then village self-sufficiency would seem to be a good option.

Thoughts about village self-sufficiency

While a small house in a village might look to be much the same in size and style as a town house – a strip of garden behind the house and the front looking onto a road – the big difference is that the space and the character of the community allows for larger structures, larger gardens, and a broader range of opportunities for keeping livestock. The space also allows for a greater degree of experimentation. If you want to go for a slower, make-do-and-mend approach that involves recycling and collecting materials, a large workshop, and a few experimental structures, then living in a village might be a good way forward.

A village is an excellent first choice if you are a nervous townie who wants to 'test the water.' Let us say that you live in town, have limited knowledge of living in the country, and yet have ambitions to try your hand at country self-sufficiency. Village properties can easily be leased for low rent, and it is also possible to rent fields and outbuildings.

We know a couple of American women, who were born and bred town folk, who wanted to try for a more rural way of living in the American Midwest. Initially, they had all sorts of preconceived notions that they might not fit in, they would be trapped, there would be no going back, the village might not be happy with two women living together, and so on. After lots of talking to friends and family, they decided to make the move in small, carefully considered stages. First, they visited their chosen village for a summer holiday, then they rented for a three-month period during winter – so that they could experience things like mud, snow, cold, and transport problems – and then they rented a low-cost village house while keeping their town house in the city. After about 18 months, they moved to the village for good. They now keep chickens, teach art at local schools, and grow most of their own food. All their fears and doubts have been washed away and they are now planning to move to a barn-type property on the village fringes.

We also know an elderly English couple who after a lifetime of city living – working in London banks and daily commuting – decided to they wanted to 'go back to the way it was.' They moved to a large plot on the edge of a village. As for being shoestring self-sufficient, while they would not really recognize the term, they grow food, store vast amounts of produce away for the winter, knit, mend, service their own small car, do their own decorating, and recycle just about every bit of plastic, string, and wood that comes their way. They tell us that in many ways life now is much the same as it was when they were kids in wartime 'Dig For Victory' Britain, the only difference being – they joke – that they don't have to worry quite so much about bombs and rationing.

The upside of village shoestring self-sufficiency

Village life can be very caring. If you are young with children, the neighbors will gather around and be supportive if there are problems. Generally, village people tend to be broadly sympathetic to shoestring living – they know about keeping chickens, growing food, woodburning stoves, log piles, farmyard-type smells and activities, and so on. There are many wild food foraging and hunting opportunities in the country (blackberries, mushrooms, crab apples, rabbits, nuts, fish, and even seashore items), which is really good if you plan to keep costs down, go organic, make wine, and generally get back to traditional country living.

There will be produce local to your area. For example, as we are surrounded by forests our logs for our stove heating are almost free for the asking. There are usually opportunities for casual farm work such as picking strawberries, grapes, or apples. Farmyard manure is very easy to come by – this is an extremely valuable resource if you intend growing your own food. It is also easier to swap, gift, sell, and trade in a small community. We know a family that makes extra cash by selling eggs at the gate, and doing gardening jobs around the village and various odd DIY jobs for neighbors. If you have kids and a local school within walking distance, then transport is easy.

The downside of village self-sufficiency

If you are a private person, village life can be can be perceived as being claustrophobic. We once lived in a village where the people were completely hostile to any sort of change; they thought of 'incomers' as intruders. Semi-rural self-sufficiency can be lonely, especially if you opt for living on the outer fringes of a large, sprawling community. Country living and darkness go hand in hand – not so good if you are nervous of the dark.

ISOLATED OFF-GRID
SELF-SUFFICIENCY

To me, the isolated off-grid option is the most exciting, the most challenging, and potentially the most rewarding. Of course, your definition of isolated will depend upon who you are and your life experiences to date, but for me the term describes a country or region of land that is off the beaten track, well away from areas of dense population, where there is plenty of space, and few, if any, neighbors.

Thoughts about the isolated off-grid option

Young or old, male or female, single or attached – you must talk your plans over with friends and family and let them know what you are doing. You must work out some sort of escape plan in case your money runs out. Are you physically and mentally prepared for such an adventure? For example, if you want to grow crops, keep stock, have a craft workshop, make a product, are you strong and fit enough for the task? If you have children and plan to move to an isolated set-up, ask yourself how you are going to tackle their education. It is easy if they are only about 10 years old, but very difficult and perhaps unfair if they are teenagers. If you plan to go with a partner, you need to know about their moods and potentially annoying idiosyncrasies. All that said, if you intend living off-grid – no neighbors, electricity, water, fuel, or shops – the primary need will be to figure out how, in the first days and weeks, you are going to get your food, do your cooking, get your water, and light your life when the sun goes down.

THE ULTIMATE SELF-SUFFICIENCY SCENARIO

A lonely farmhouse snuggled away in a dip of lush fields and meadows, some sort of fisherman's shack on a beach, a mountain cabin in Canada, an old farmhouse in rural France complete with a vineyard, a long and lonely stretch of seashore in New Zealand – no matter how you see your perfect self-sufficient set-up in your mind's eye, there are a few requirements that your chosen property must have if it is going to work out. The ideal plot must be the right character to suit your needs, it must be the right size, it must be correctly orientated to the sun, it must have good water, all the legal rights must be defined and to your advantage, it must be free from pollution, contamination, and flood, and, most important of all in these troubled times, it must be situated in a country that is politically and economically stable.

A good first step is to draw up a must-have list. So, for example, if it must have a lake, an orchard, and river running through, then detail this in your list and don't settle for anything less. The biggest mistake when looking for properties is the temptation to go for a place that is almost but not quite right. You might get to see the right house, the right land, the right everything – almost – but if there is no water in high summer, or there is some sort of ongoing dispute about land ownership, for example, then it will not work out. Experience tells us that if you settle for 'almost right' then the missing factors will either instantly crash the project or at the very least wear away at you over the years.

IDEAL RURAL PLOT

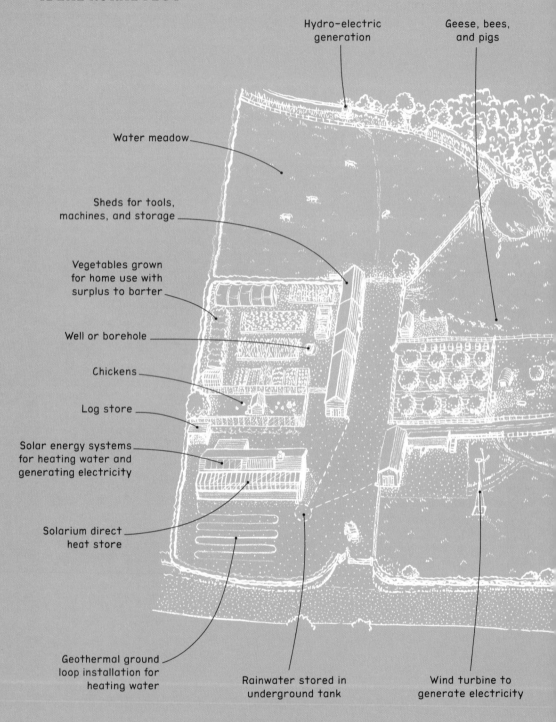

Hydro-electric generation

Geese, bees, and pigs

Water meadow

Sheds for tools, machines, and storage

Vegetables grown for home use with surplus to barter

Well or borehole

Chickens

Log store

Solar energy systems for heating water and generating electricity

Solarium direct heat store

Geothermal ground loop installation for heating water

Rainwater stored in underground tank

Wind turbine to generate electricity

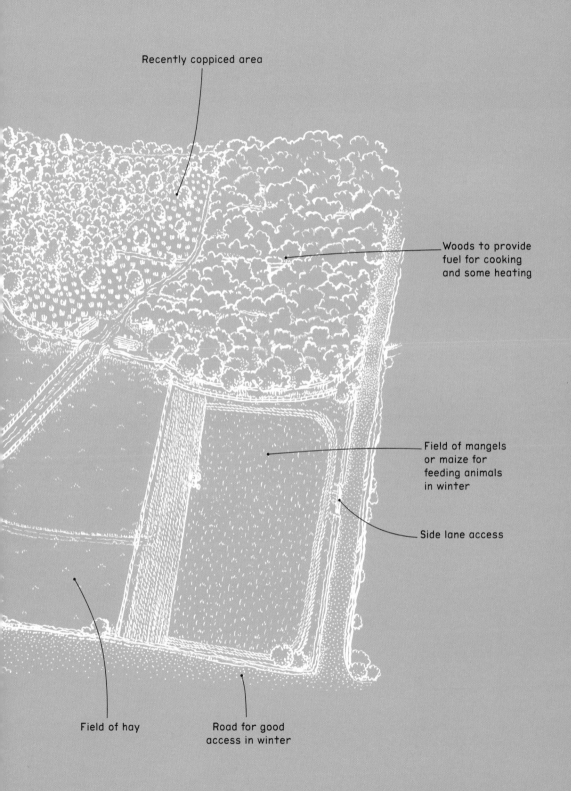

Recently coppiced area

Woods to provide
fuel for cooking
and some heating

Field of mangels
or maize for
feeding animals
in winter

Side lane access

Field of hay

Road for good
access in winter

Your basic needs

Draw up a list of your minimum requirements – number of hectares/acres, type of house, number of outbuildings, climate, soil type, and any other relevant factor. Decide just how much you are prepared to veer away from the list and then go out looking for it.

Orientation

Correct orientation is vital. No matter where in the world you have in mind to settle, the best you can hope for is a plot of slightly sloping ground that looks to the sun at midday. Such a site will get the best of the sun and be well drained. Even if you like woods and mountains, try to avoid a site that is on the shadow side of a vast stand of trees or mountains, or is directly in the path of prevailing winds.

Water

Good water is essential. If the property is off-grid, then there must be a supply of water – a clean stream or river, a well, or a borehole. You must know that the water is still available in high summer. If you own the land but not the river/stream, then you must ensure that you have the right to extract water. Nevertheless, remember that while you need good water you don't want a property that floods.

Legal ownership and rights

You must make sure that all rights are to your advantage. Never take people's word about boundaries, rights of way, or other legal matters – always make sure that everything is yours by legal right. Avoid properties that have odd clauses; for example, one of our properties stated in the small print that we could not run a fairground, have a caravan, or trade in any way.

Pollution and contamination

This is a difficult one. The best you can do is ask your legal advisor to make checks. You don't want to be buying dirty water, ground contaminated with chemicals, land that sits to the windward side of a chemical works, or land that was/is/could be a dumping ground for waste.

Political and economical stability

We know a couple who set up house and home on an island in the Mediterranean. It was wonderful until a disgruntled neighboring country took the half of the island that they had long considered to be rightfully theirs. The couple lost everything.

AN AUTONOMOUS HOUSE

An autonomous house – independent, self-contained, and stand-alone – makes its own electricity, collects its own water, deals with its own waste, and grows its own food, all at little or no running cost. While the autonomous house uses renewable energy systems like solar water heaters, solar voltaic panels, and wind turbines, its efficiency to a great extent depends upon the occupants modifying their needs. Although many people are happy to nudge or even completely change their lifestyle in order to make the various systems work – they think of it as an exciting challenge – others think that *modifying* equates with *lowering* and will not accept it.

Autonomous systems and options

Grey water A grey water system – really no more than an arrangement of underground tanks complete with in-and-out pipes and pumps – stores water from baths and showers and reuses it to flush toilets.

Water from a well or borehole This is good if a house has a tried and trusted well, but not so good if you have to sink a borehole. Personal experience tells us that drilling a borehole is both expensive and uncertain.

Rainwater In some regions it is possible to store and use rainwater. A modern system needs storage tanks, pumps, and purification.

Sewage The autonomous house has a non-water composting toilet that turns human feces into a dry, odorless, friable, peat-like product that can safely be used on the vegetable garden. In this way the human excrement becomes a valuable resource.

Electricity

Reduce usage The autonomous house uses low-usage items like led lighting and superefficient electric white goods to dramatically reduce demand.

Photovoltaic (PV) solar panels Solar panels turn sunlight into electricity. We have a roof-mounted array of six panels that powers our lights and small items like the television and computers. Solar cells are 'passive' in the sense that they have no moving parts.

Wind turbine This is a good option for a windy area where there are no high buildings or trees. The ideal is to have a turbine running alongside solar power – solar for sunny days and the turbine when it is cloudy but windy. The downside with a turbine is that it needs regular servicing – lowering the mast, checking lubrication, looking at wires and batteries, and so on. In an off-grid house, the power is stored in banks of batteries.

Solar and passive space heating The autonomous house uses a mix of solar collectors and Trombe walls (walls designed to store heat from the sun). For maximum efficiency, solar systems must look to the sun at midday, the building must be highly insulated, and the structure must incorporate thermal mass to store daytime heat.

Woodburning stoves for heating The autonomous house has a woodburning stove running alongside solar and passive systems. Stoves are easy to use and perceived as giving a 'cozy' heat. Our woodburning stove provides both heat and hot water.

Solar water heating Solar water heaters save large amounts of fuel. Their efficiency can be increased simply by doing laundry-type chores on sunny days. Our 'microsolar' system gives us as much hot water as we can manage. In summer the solar heater does all the work, while in the winter the stove and the solar heater work together.

Food production The ideal autonomous set-up includes a no-dig vegetable garden, a small amount of forest coppicing, and traditional mixed stock farming. We produce vegetables, eggs, and honey. Experience tells us that 280 m² (3,000 sq. ft) of good land, plus an integral greenhouse, will feed a vegetarian family of four.

AUTONOMOUS HOUSE FACING THE SUN

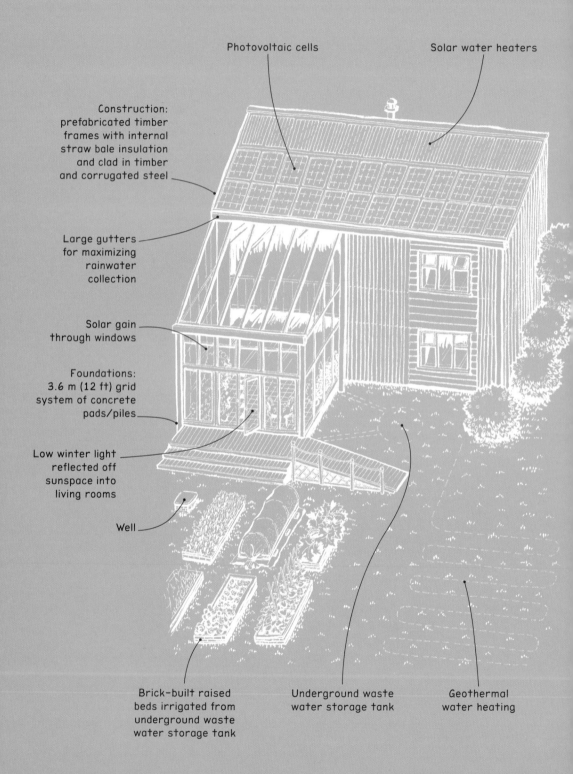

Photovoltaic cells

Solar water heaters

Construction: prefabricated timber frames with internal straw bale insulation and clad in timber and corrugated steel

Large gutters for maximizing rainwater collection

Solar gain through windows

Foundations: 3.6 m (12 ft) grid system of concrete pads/piles

Low winter light reflected off sunspace into living rooms

Well

Brick-built raised beds irrigated from underground waste water storage tank

Underground waste water storage tank

Geothermal water heating

SHOESTRING HOUSE

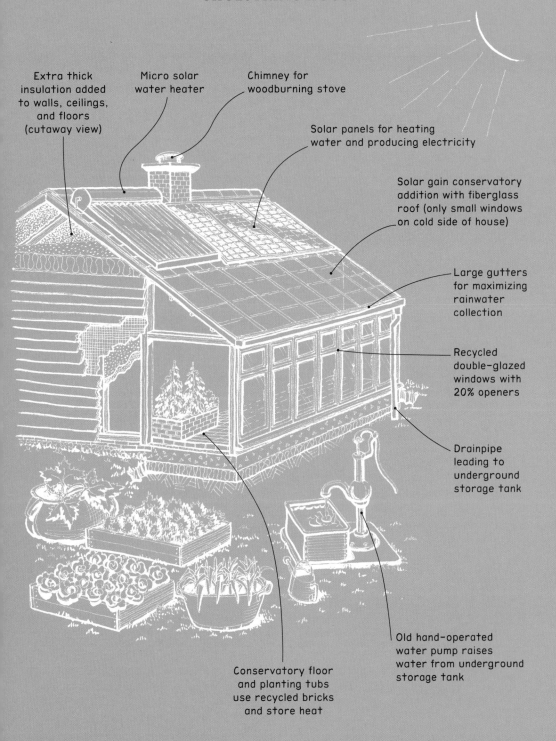

Extra thick insulation added to walls, ceilings, and floors (cutaway view)

Micro solar water heater

Chimney for woodburning stove

Solar panels for heating water and producing electricity

Solar gain conservatory addition with fiberglass roof (only small windows on cold side of house)

Large gutters for maximizing rainwater collection

Recycled double-glazed windows with 20% openers

Drainpipe leading to underground storage tank

Old hand-operated water pump raises water from underground storage tank

Conservatory floor and planting tubs use recycled bricks and store heat

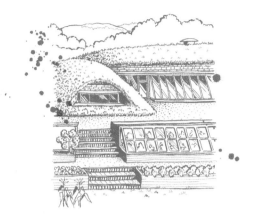

EXTREME SHOESTRING
SELF-SUFFICIENCY

From time to time we are asked whether it is possible to achieve extreme self-sufficiency. If we take it that this means building an extreme low-energy home (say an earth sheltered house) and then managing all the food, clothes, and waste on site, with little or no contact with the outside world – like pioneer homesteaders going out west – I believe it could only work in a set-up where the occupants live a tight, self-reliant lifestyle that involves a mix of some sort of subsistence farming and a small amount of bartering or gifting.

We know of two extreme self-sufficiency set-ups. In the first case, a super-rich ex-popstar and his wife live a kind of semi-hermit existence in a vast autonomous house in the middle of a huge estate, where they grow organic food and keep bees. In the second case, an old guy lives in a small wooden shack miles from anywhere on the edge of the marshes and grows his own food, catches fish, beachcombs, and sells stuff at the gate.

As for the original question, I would say it *is* possible to achieve extreme self-sufficiency, but you must ask yourself the following: are you strongly self-reliant and resilient, and can you imagine yourself leading a lonely, reclusive, survivalist sort of life?

FOOD

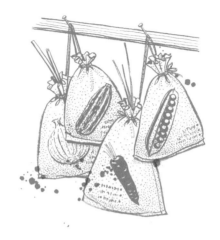

NO-DIG
SELF-SUFFICIENCY

If no-dig (or do-nothing) gardening is a method of organic food gardening, and shoestring has to do with recycling and make-do-and-mend, if we wrap the two notions together with self-sufficiency we have a form of growing food where every aspect involves saving and recycling. The raised beds are made from salvaged materials, the growing medium is made from materials like leaf mold, kitchen compost, and farmyard manure, and, most important of all, the seeds are obtained by saving.

Saving your own seed

If you live a good distance from neighbors and have had enough of flashy seed catalogues, seed packets getting bigger and more brightly illustrated, and prices going up and the number of seeds going down, then keep reading. Saving your own seed will not only dramatically cut your spending, it will ensure that you get your favorite heirloom varieties – all the varieties that our grandparents grew through many generations by saving seed from what they considered to be the strongest and most flavorsome vegetables. When saving seeds, always take them from mature, healthy, non-hybrid varieties. While seeds like beans, peas, lettuces, tomatoes, sweet peppers, and aubergines (eggplants) are easy to germinate, ones like cucumbers, melons, and pumpkins are a bit trickier. With biennials like carrots, beets, onions, and brassicas, you will need to grow the plants to their second year before collecting the seeds. See the various growing entries for more details.

THE NO-DIG METHOD

The way it was

When I was a kid, gardeners used to slog through the autumn digging their plots. Some observed that although digging certainly removed perennial weed roots and made the plot look neat, it brought dormant seeds to the surface where they germinated, and it shifted valuable surface organic material to a deeper level where it was not used.

No-dig explained

In nature, vegetation falls to the ground, worms drag the organic matter into the soil, microscopic soil life works on the organic matter, more vegetation falls, and so on. The no-dig raised bed method mimics nature: mulches leave the soil more or less untouched so that micro- and macrobiotic organisms can achieve a balanced, active, and dynamic environment, this environment in turn nurtures and feeds the plants, the thriving plants transfer a portion of their carbon energy to the soil, the microbes that benefit from this plant energy in turn convert available organic substances into the mineral elements that the plants need to thrive, and so on in a continuous cycle.

Advantages of no-dig

* The size and layout of the raised beds and paths can be shaped to suit your garden, your unique growing pleasures, and your physical needs. For example, we dislike bending and stretching, so we have built extra deep beds that we can work from all sides.

* The structure and make-up of the growing medium can be swiftly modified to suit specific plants – deep and rich for runner beans, a sandier medium for onions, and so on.

* The box structure of the raised beds allows us to easily build up mulches to protect leeks, blanch celery, or to 'earth up' potatoes.

* The box structure allows us to easily protect the crops with windbreaks, nets, plastic sheet, fleece, or whatever is appropriate.

How the no-dig raised bed method works

* The 90 cm (3 ft) square, 23 cm (9 in) deep, wooden bed is set in place, the weeds are removed from the base soil, and the depth of the bed is layered up with shredded newspaper and card topped off with layers of mulch – such as well-rotted manure, kitchen waste, leaf mold, spent mushroom compost.

* You sow and plant your vegetables.

* Worms, insects, and microbes break the mulch layers down and incorporate them into the base soil.

* The worm, insect, and microbe activity creates tunnels and cavities that provide aeration and drainage.

* The waste created by the worms, insects, and microbes binds the soil crumbs together which in turn creates a natural, undisturbed environment that allows plant roots to thrive and the population of insects and microbes to build up.

* These conditions encourage the build-up of beneficial rather than harmful soil fungi.

* As and when you see weeds, pull up and burn deep-rooted perennials, and smother all the others with yet another layer of mulch made from kitchen compost, well-rotted farmyard manure, or whatever comes to hand.

VEGETABLE-GROWING BASICS

The definitive shoestring no-dig vegetable garden

The ideal no-dig vegetable garden, especially if you want to save your own seeds, is sheltered on the windward side by trees or hills, the ground is very slightly inclined so that the sun strikes it at midday, and the whole area is located in a rural setting well away from neighbors. Our raised beds are all located together on one patch, but there is no reason why your beds cannot be scattered so that they best fill the available space.

Raised beds

Although the ideal is to have 90 cm (3 ft) square wooden beds made from 23 cm (9 in) wide board, they can be made from just about any salvaged material that comes to hand. We have beds made from a water tank, old cattle troughs, builder's bags, and dustbins.

Layering the growing medium

Once you have set the beds in place, scrape the weeds off the base ground, cover the ground with newspaper and/or cardboard, and then layer up the depth within the bed with a mix of leaf mold, straw/hay, kitchen and garden compost, manure and/or whatever composted vegetable-based material is available.

Well-rotted farmyard manure

Although we use a mix of horse and geese manure, you can of course use manure from cows, turkeys, or any other suitable animal or bird. A good shoestring option is to keep chickens so that you get both eggs and manure.

Crop rotation

The ideal is to rotate your growing plan so that you plant different crops on different beds: brassicas in the first year, legumes and salad in the second year, roots in the third year, and then back round to brassicas in the fourth year. We sometimes, if necessary, rotate half beds, or completely replace or modify the growing medium.

Mid-winter

Ongoing tasks Sort out items like string, pots, plastic, netting, and fleece. Set seed potatoes to sprout and make plans. Remove weeds and spread mulch of well-rotted manure on beds.

Sowing and planting Sow broad beans in beds and pots, and onions, leeks, and radishes in protected beds.

Cropping Pick Brussels, winter cabbage, last of the carrots, celery, chicory, and anything else that is ready.

Late winter

Ongoing tasks Clean up around the beds. In cold weather, cover beds with fleece or nets. Prepare a nursery bed in a protected corner. Remove weeds, add mulch, and put debris on the compost heap.

Sowing and planting Plant artichokes and shallots. Sow early peas and more broad beans. Sow carrots, lettuces, and radishes in beds and protect with glass/plastic/mats. Raise leek, cucumber, onion, and tomato seedlings in protected warm beds.

Cropping Pick Brussels, winter cabbage, last of the carrots, celery, chicory, and anything else that is ready.

Early spring

Ongoing tasks Weed paths and mend beds. Remove deep-rooted perennials and add mulch.

Sowing and planting Sow hardy seeds like lettuces and parsnips out of doors. Sow spinach, broccoli, leeks, onions, peas, celery, tomatoes, and marrows under glass or in protected beds.

Cropping Pick sprouts, cabbage and cauliflower.

Mid-spring

Ongoing tasks Watch out for birds, slugs, and mice on strawberry beds. Keep pulling large weeds and putting down mulches to control surface weeds. Reduce the number of sprouts on seed potatoes. Cover selected beds at night. Thin seedlings. Draw the soil and mulch up around potatoes.

Sowing and planting Sow most items in the open. Sow maincrop potatoes, onions, radishes, maincrop carrots, beet, salsify and scorzonera, endives, more lettuces, peas, and spinach. Plant out hardened-off seedlings. Sow runner beans, marrows, and courgettes (zucchini) under glass.

Cropping Pick beet leaf and broccoli.

Late spring

Ongoing tasks Watch for bad weather and be ready to protect tender seedlings with glass, plastic sheet, net screens, or whatever seems to be appropriate. Remove blackfly on beans, set twigs among the peas, put mulch on selected beds, reduce the number of runners on the strawberries, water seedlings, remove large weeds, and keep spreading mulch to smother small weeds. Prepare more seedbeds. Spread mulch around potatoes and more advanced vegetables.

Sowing and planting Plant out hardy seedlings. Sow tender vegetables in vacant beds. Sow French, runner, and brown beans in the open. Sow more peas, endives, radishes, summer spinach, and anything else that takes your fancy. Plant out Brussels, broccoli, cucumbers, and anything else that suits your needs.

Cropping Pick beet leaf, broccoli, early beetroot, early carrots, cucumbers under cover, endives, and anything else that is ready.

Early summer

Ongoing tasks Bring in fresh manure, well-rotted manure, and spent mushroom compost. Keep everything well watered. Spread mulches around turnips and on vacant beds. Put nets over fruit, remove weak raspberry canes, clean out empty beds, and keep lifting deep-rooted weeds and spreading mulch. Use twigs to support runner beans and peas. Dig up potatoes.

Sowing and planting Plant out seedlings and sow succession crops like endives, lettuces, and radishes.

Cropping Pick anything that takes your fancy.

Mid-summer

Ongoing tasks Support plants that look hot and droopy. Gather ripe soft fruit. Cut and dry mint and other herbs. Spread manure mulch. Look at the tomatoes and pinch out and feed as necessary. Lift potatoes. Weed, water, and mulch between crops and make sure that the polytunnel/greenhouse and beds are open to the air. Weed after lifting potatoes and mulch up around maincrop potatoes.

Sowing and planting Plant out celery and things like cabbage, sprouts, and broccoli.

Cropping Continue picking, eating, and storing.

Late summer

Ongoing tasks Order seeds and/or save your own. Bottle, can, dry, and freeze produce. Bend over the necks of onions. Dry herbs. Pinch out the tops of tomatoes. Use nets to protect delicate fruit against birds. Plant out new strawberry beds. Continue weeding and mulching.

Sowing and planting Make more sowings of endives, radishes, spinach, onions, and anything else that fits the season. Sow lettuces and salad crops under cover. Sow cabbages for spring planting.

Cropping Continue picking, eating, and storing. Dry more herbs; gather beans, tomatoes, and fruit as and when they are ready.

Early autumn

Ongoing tasks Protect from frosts. Lift and store roots. Earth up celery and leeks and mulch with straw or hay. Remove and destroy caterpillars. Prune raspberries and blanche endives. Weed and mulch as soon as you have cleared the crops.

Sowing and planting Plant out spring cabbages. Look at your seeds and sow if possible.

Cropping Lift potatoes and onions. Gather runner beans. Lift and store roots. Gather and store fruit as it ripens. Continue picking, eating, and storing.

Mid-autumn

Ongoing tasks Clear the ground and put debris on the compost heap. Clean up paths. Weed and mulch vacant beds and protect from frost and wind. Thin onions.

Sowing and planting Plant rhubarb and fruit trees. Sow peas in protected beds. Sow salad crops under glass. Plant out seedlings. Sow early peas in warm areas.

Cropping Gather the remaining tomatoes. Lift and pick things like celeriac and carrots.

Late autumn

Ongoing tasks Watch out for frost and protect as needed. Clean up leaves and debris and mulch vacant beds. Remove bean and pea sticks and poles.

Sowing and planting Sow broad beans in a sheltered bed.

Cropping Lift and store root crops. Cut and lift crops as needed.

Early winter

Ongoing tasks Protect against frosts. Clean the tools and the shed, and weed and mulch beds as they become vacant. Heap mulch around the peas and ensure that stored vegetables are in good order.

Sowing and planting Plant broad beans in mild weather. Sow salad crops under glass and protect as needed.

Cropping Pick the last of the beet leaf. Pick Brussels, winter cabbages, last of the carrots, celery, chicory, and anything else that is ready.

SOWING, POTTING, AND PLANTING

Seeds can be sown directly in position in the beds at the correct spacing and depth, in specially prepared nursery beds, or in trays, pots, and containers in the greenhouse. Once the seeds have grown into easy-to-handle seedlings, they can be potted on into larger containers and then planted out in the beds, or they can be planted directly out into the beds. Your chosen procedure will depend upon the type of seeds, your location and climate, the time of year, and your experience last time around.

Sowing directly in beds

Large, easy-to-handle seeds like beans, peas, sweetcorn, and potatoes can be planted directly in place, at the correct spacing and depth, in the beds. Small seeds like brassicas and root crops like carrots and parsnips can be sown in little groups in a V-section drill and then thinned to the best plants at a later stage.

Sowing in nursery seedbeds

Small seeds like brassicas can be sown in V-section drills and then lifted and planted when they are big and strong enough to handle. This does not work for most root crops.

Sowing in the greenhouse

Seeds like brassicas, beans, and peas can be sown in trays, pots, and lengths of plastic gutter in the greenhouse and planted out later. We sow our peas in a gutter and plant them out when they are too big and tough for the birds and mice. To increase our success rate, we sow seeds like beans both directly in the beds and in pots in the greenhouse.

Potting on

Having sown small seeds in trays and pots in the greenhouse, the seedlings generally need to be potted on into larger and larger pots before being finally planted out.

Planting out

Once seeds have been sown in pots and trays in the greenhouse and the seedlings maybe potted on into larger pots, they can be planted out in their final position in the beds.

HOW TO DEAL WITH PESTS AND DISEASES

Growing food can be a long battle against all the things that threaten to blight and blast your crops. Mice, moles, voles, rats, cats, rabbits, squirrels, snakes, slugs, snails, and birds want to eat them. Flies, bugs, and butterflies want to lay eggs on them, and these will in turn become greedy grubs, caterpillars, and larvae that will also want to eat the leaves, bore holes, and generally damage leaves, stalks, flowers, roots, and shoots. Microscopic viruses, molds, messes, and mildews want to attack the plants. Last but not least, weather-related problems, such as too much sun, heavy rain squalls, extreme frosts, heavy snow, and howling winds, can cause physical damage.

The challenge for us as organic, shoestring, self-sufficient food growers is to work out how we can win the battle without resorting to some sort of all-out chemical warfare, without spending a lot of money and without doing damage to the environment.

Gill and I have developed a five-pronged approach. We start by planting extra in the certain knowledge that nature will take its cut. We use homemade organic sprays, such as chopped tomato leaves soaked in water that we spray on things like aphids, and a chopped garlic and oil mix that is a great antibacterial, antifungal, and insect pest spray. We use physical barriers such as fleece, netting, and plastic sheet to protect against insects, animals, and weather. We use lots of hand gathering to dispose of caterpillars and slugs. Finally, we use all manner of traps and tricks to deter or catch pests such as mice.

If we stay with the analogy that gardening is a battle, we don't want to annihilate our enemies so much as come to some sort of reasonable truce. The truth is that the more wildlife we have in the garden the better it is for all of us. The birds will certainly eat some part of our pea crop, but in return not only do they eat things like slugs, snails, and greenfly, but their very presence deters all kinds of other pests. The give-and-take truce seems to be working out all round.

Insects and bugs

Earwigs
* **Problem** Lots of holes in leaves
* **Line of attack** Trap in upturned pots filled with straw, and spray plants with garlic and pepper mix

Aphids
* **Problem** Sticky mess indicating an infestation
* **Line of attack** Drench with garlic and pepper spray
* **Follow-up** Burn debris

Cabbage caterpillars
* **Problem** holes, eggs and caterpillars
* **Line of attack** cover with nets to keep off the butterflies
* **Follow-up** collect and destroy eggs and caterpillars

Diamond back moths
* **Problem** Caterpillars eating the leaves
* **Line of attack** Cover with nets to keep off the moths
* **Follow-up** Collect the caterpillars by hand

Flea beetles
* **Problem** Small holes in leaves
* **Line of attack** Drench the plants with garlic and oil spray
* **Follow-up** Collect and burn debris

Asparagus beetles
* **Problem** Damage to leaves and stems
* **Line of attack** Collect and destroy the beetles and grubs
* **Follow-up** Collect and burn all the debris

Celery leaf miners
* **Problem** Blisters and shriveling leaves
* **Line of attack** Drench plants with soft soap solution
* **Follow-up** Collect and kill larvae and earth up around plant

Black bean aphids
* **Problem** Mess of sticky black aphids on leaves and stems
* **Line of attack** Drench the plants with a mix of soft soap and white mineral oil
* **Follow-up** Do your best to encourage predatory ladybugs and other aphid-eating wildlife

Pea and bean weevils
* **Problem** Bite and nibble around the edges of the leaves
* **Line of attack** Puff organic derris dust around the leaves
* **Follow-up** Collect and burn all the debris

Pea thrips
* **Problem** Silvery brown, misshapen pods
* **Line of attack** Spray the plants with insecticidal soap
* **Follow-up** Avoid the problem by burning all the debris

Pea moths
* **Problem** Peas with holes and maggots
* **Line of attack** Guard against the problem by ringing the bed with a barrier of fine fleece or netting and drench the plants with a natural soap spray
* **Follow-up** Burn all the debris after cropping

Green capsid bugs
* **Problem** Holes in leaves and deformed growth
* **Line of attack** Drench with organic spray

Red spider mites
* **Problem** Veins of leaves turn yellow-red-brown and leaves have a dusty covering
* **Line of attack** Drench with neem oil (an organic pesticide), or with a homemade coriander and oil spray
* **Follow-up** Scrape up and burn ground debris

Greenhouse whitefly
* **Problem** Shows as a sticky mess of eggs on the underside of leaves and as deformed leaves
* **Line of attack** Spray with insect soap or dust with seaweed powder
* **Follow-up** Spray the empty greenhouse in winter with a thin oil-tar wash

Diseases

Powdery mildew
* **Problem** Flour-like dusting on leaves
* **Line of attack** Drench with milk and water spray

Mosaic virus
* **Problem** Spotted green-yellow areas on leaves, and eventual complete plant failure
* **Line of attack** Drench plants with a tobacco and water spray
* **Follow-up** Burn badly damaged plants and look for a resistant variety next time

Potato blight
* **Problem** Black and brown spots on leaves, and scabby soft potatoes that rot in the ground
* **Line of attack** Cut and burn foliage and crop what is left
* **Follow-up** Clear beds and burn debris; next time try resistant varieties on new beds in a different part of the garden

Potato leaf roll virus
* **Problem** Rolled edges and leaf fall
* **Line of attack** Drench with an anti-aphid mix
* **Follow-up** Collect and burn debris, use a resistant variety next time, and plant in a different plot

Bean halo blight
* **Problem** Squashy rusty scabs on the leaves and eventual plant failure
* **Line of attack** Drench with an organic spray
* **Follow-up** Pull and burn plants and next time plant disease-resistant varieties in new beds

Celery heart rot
* **Problem** Soft brown rot at the center of the plant
* **Line of attack** Pull out plants and eat what you can
* **Follow-up** Avoid the problem next time by binding the growing plant with raffia and gradually earthing up so that the center of the plant stays dry

Rust
* **Problem** Brown, scabby leaves
* **Line of attack** Spray with garlic oil or neem oil
* **Follow-up** Burn all the debris at the end of the season

Smut
* **Problem** Sooty-looking mess on the leaves that smears on contact
* **Line of attack** Wash off with a thin soapy mix and/or drench with neem oil
* **Follow-up** Burn all the debris at the end of the season and next time plant resistant varieties in a different bed

Tomato leaf mold
* **Problem** Yellow-brown leaves and wilting plant
* **Line of attack** Remove damaged leaves and drench plants with a solution of water, baking soda, vegetable oil and dishwashing liquid
* **Follow-up** Make sure plants are well away from potatoes and burn debris as soon as the plants have cropped

Bird and beast pests

Slugs and snails
* **Problem** Slimy damage to leaves and stalks
* **Line of attack** Remove by hand and destroy
* **Follow-up** Ring the beds with copper wire stripped and nailed to the top edge of the board (it seems to work, but we don't know why!)

Mice and voles
* **Problem** They pull up and eat seeds and pods, and ruin crops like strawberries
* **Line of attack** Sow peas in the greenhouse in lengths of plastic gutter, wait until they are about 5–7.5 cm (2–3 in) high, then slide the young plants into place in the beds
* **Follow-up** As soon as you spot the problem, ring the beds with nets and set mousetraps

Rats
* **Problem** They can strip a crop overnight
* **Line of attack** Ring the crop with nets and set traps
* **Follow-up** Make sure your kitchen compost heap does not attract the rats, and think about getting a cat

Rabbits
* **Problem** They can completely ruin a vegetable plot
* **Line of attack** Ring the plot with rabbit netting
* **Follow-up** We shoot the rabbits and feed them to our dogs

Squirrels
* **Problem** Squirrels will eat most things
* **Line of attack** Set fine nets and noise makers
* **Follow-up** Get a small, noisy dog

Cats
* **Problem** Neighbors' cats use our plots as a latrine
* **Line of attack** Cover beds with nets and a mesh of fine cotton and maybe fit a water spray
* **Follow-up** Get a small, noisy dog

Birds
* **Problem** They eat berries and peas and cause damage to tender green plants like cabbages
* **Line of attack** Protect with nets, or plant extra crops in the knowledge that some birds will eat insect pests

Homemade organic sprays

Garlic and pepper Add 3 cloves crushed garlic and 1 tablespoon vegetable oil to 3 tablespoons hot pepper sauce and let it stand overnight. Next add the mix to 1 small spoon of unscented washing-up liquid and add it all to 4 cups of water. This mix can be sprayed direct.

Garlic and oil Add 3 cloves crushed garlic to 2 small spoons mineral oil, let it sit for a day, then strain and add to 1 pint water. Shake and add 1 small spoonful of washing-up liquid. When you come to spray, add 2 tablespoons of this mix to 1 pint of water.

Tomato leaf Soak 2 cups chopped tomato leaves in 2 cups water overnight and strain. When you come to spray, use 1 measure of the mix to 1 measure of water.

Insecticidal soap Mix 1 small spoon pure unscented soap into 1 quart water. This dissolves insects like aphids, mites, thrips, and a whole range of scale insects.

Neem oil Various mixes of neem seed oil repel cabbage worm, aphids, and moth larvae, and also control powdery mildew and rust. 30 ml (1 fl oz) neem oil and a few drops of soap liquid mixed into 4.5 liters (1 gallon) water make a good spray to treat all manner of mold and mites.

Seaweed Applied dry or as a mulch will enrich the ground and keep insects at bay. Seaweed also repels slugs.

Tobacco Soak 1 cup tobacco leaves or butts and 1 small spoon natural soap in 4.5 liters (1 gallon) water. Strain to spray.

Aphid mix Mix 1 small spoon soft soap and 1 cup vegetable oil in water, and spray.

Baking soda Mix 1 tablespoon each of baking soda, vegetable oil, and dishwashing liquid with 4.5 liters (1 gallon) of water, and spray.

Stinging nettles Soak 1 liter (2 pints) of nettles in water for two weeks, strain and mix 1 part of the brew into 7 parts water.

BRASSICAS

Sprouting broccoli

Homegrown sprouting white and purple broccoli is tender and tasty. We sow both in a seedbed and under glass.

Saving seed To avoid cross-pollination, your garden must be isolated. Grow the best plants on to their second year, cut the tops off late in the season, grow the plants on through to the next year, and collect and dry the seed at the end of the second season.

Sowing in a seedbed Mid- to late spring – sow thinly 6 mm (¼ in) deep in rows 15 cm (6 in) apart.

Sowing under glass Sow early spring onwards in deep trays/pots in the greenhouse.

Thinning outdoors Thin to about 5 cm (2 in) apart.

Planting out When the seedlings are strong enough to handle, plant them out in dibbed holes about 30 cm (1 ft) apart, with 5–6 plants to a 90 cm (3 ft) square bed.

Protection Use fleece or fine net to protect from birds, butterflies, and strong sun.

Care Remove yellow leaves and debris and add a mulch to keep down weeds and hold in moisture.

Cropping In the following spring, first crop the heads and then the sideshoots.

Brussels sprouts

For best eating, sprouts need to be young, fresh, and lightly steamed. We prefer to sow in deep trays under glass.

Saving seed Your garden must be isolated. Cut down to a stump late in the season, grow on to the next year, and collect and dry the seed at the end of the second season.

Sowing under glass Sow early spring onwards – three seeds per pot.

Planting out When the seedlings are strong enough to handle, plant them out in dibbed holes, with 5–6 plants to a 90 cm (3 ft) square bed.

Protection Cover with fleece or fine draped net to protect from birds, butterflies, and strong sun.

Care In windy areas, stake the plants up; remove debris, and add a mulch to keep down weeds and hold in moisture.

Cropping In early winter, first pick the head of the plant and then, starting at the bottom of the stem, pick the sprouts.

Cabbages

By working through the varieties, homegrown cabbages can be eaten all year round. We sow both in the seedbed and in the greenhouse.

Saving seed As most members of the cabbage family are biennial and easily cross-pollinate, you must be 1.5 km (1 mile) away from other gardens. Grow and mature in the first season and overwinter before setting seed in the spring of the second year – see Brussels sprouts and broccoli.

Sowing in a seedbed Mid- to late spring – sow thinly 18 mm (¾ in) deep, in rows 15 cm (6 in) apart.

Sowing under glass Sow early spring onwards in deep trays/pots in the greenhouse.

Thinning outdoors Thin to about 5 cm (2 in) apart.

Planting out When the bed-grown seedlings and the seeds grown under glass are strong enough to handle, plant them into dibbed holes about 30 cm (1 ft) apart, with 5–6 plants to a 90 cm (3 ft) square bed.

Protection Use fleece or fine net to protect from birds and butterflies. Remove caterpillars by hand.

Care Remove yellow leaves and burn debris. Add a mulch to keep down weeds and hold in moisture. Use another plot next time.

Cropping Cut as needed.

Cauliflowers

Depending upon the variety, cauliflowers can be eaten from mid-summer through to early autumn and the following summer.

Saving seed Grow a few plants on to overwinter. Let them flower and seed in the second year. Pick the seed pods when they are mature and dry.

Sowing in a seedbed Mid- to late spring – sow thinly 12 mm (½ in) deep in rows and 20 cm (8 in) apart.

Sowing under glass Sow early spring onwards in deep trays/pots in the greenhouse.

Thinning outdoors Thin to about 5 cm (2 in) apart.

Planting out When the bed-grown seedlings and the seeds grown under glass are strong enough to handle, plant them in dibbed and puddled holes about 30–45 cm (12–18 in) apart, with 5–6 plants to a 90 cm (3 ft) square bed.

Protection Use fleece or fine net to protect from birds, butterflies, and strong sun; cover the head in extreme wet or dry weather.

Care Remove and burn all yellow leaves and debris. Add a mulch to keep down weeds and hold in moisture.

Cropping Crop when the heads are white and firm.

Kale

Picked when it is young and tender, homegrown kale or curly kale is easy to grow, hardy, and altogether delicious.

Saving seed You must be well away from other gardens. Grow the best plants on to overwinter and collect the seedpods in the second season.

Sowing directly in the raised bed Late spring to early summer – sow a pinch of seed 12 mm (½ in) deep, directly in position in the raised bed, with 5–6 plants to a 90 cm (3 ft) square bed.

Thinning Thin to one best plant at each position.

Protection Use fleece or fine net to protect from birds and butterflies.

Care Collect and burn debris and add a mulch to keep down weeds and hold in moisture.

Cropping From autumn to late spring, first eat the crown and then the sideshoots.

SALAD LEAVES

Beet leaf

Beet leaf, also called spinach beet, perpetual spinach, and chard, can be grown and harvested for a good part of the year.

Saving seed As beet is wind-pollinated and the seed light in weight and easily cross-pollinated, you must be at least 8 km (5 miles) away from your nearest neighbors. Wait until the seedheads start to blacken and then tie a paper bag over the head to catch the seed. If you sow the parent plants in spring, the seeds can be in the bag by autumn.

Sowing in a seedbed Mid- to late spring – sow a pinch 6 mm (¼ in) deep, in a 23 cm (9 in) grid pattern.

Thinning Thin to a single best plant at each station.

Protection Hardy, so needs little protection.

Care Remove yellow leaves and debris. Layer mulch around the plants to keep down weeds and hold in moisture.

Cropping Pick young leaves from early to mid-autumn onwards.

Chicory

Although chicory is a long-winded item to grow, it neatly fills the gap in winter when other salad crops are thin on the ground. It can be cropped from autumn onwards.

Saving seed Only possible if your garden is isolated. Leave the center of the plant to overwinter, flower and produce seeds. Tie a paper bag over the seedhead to collect the seeds.

Sowing in raised beds Mid-spring – sow a pinch of seed 12 mm (½ in) deep, in a 20 cm (8 in) grid pattern.

Thinning out When the seedlings are strong enough to handle, thin them to one strong plant at each station.

Protection Cover with fine draped net to protect from birds. Remove slugs by hand.

Care When the tops are dying down in autumn, lift and trim the roots and store in a box in dry sand. In spring, plant four roots at a time in a large pot in the greenhouse, water, and cover with black plastic.

Cropping In 3–4 weeks, the roots will produce the characteristic bud-like chicons.

Land cress and salad leaves

If you work through the various varieties, you can be eating lamb's lettuce, rocket, curled cress, and land cress from late autumn to spring onwards. We sow both in the seedbed and in the greenhouse.

Saving seed Wait until the plants have flowered and gather the seeds as they ripen.

Sowing in raised beds Late spring to early summer – sow a pinch of seeds 6 mm (¼ in) deep, in a 15–20 cm (6–8 in) grid pattern.

Thinning outdoors Thin to the best plant at each station.

Protection Use fleece or fine net to protect from birds and flea beetles. Remove slugs and snails by hand.

Care Add a mulch to keep down weeds and hold in moisture. Water regularly.

Cropping Keep cutting young tender leaves to encourage growth.

Lettuces

A good fresh crisp young lettuce is perfect with bread and cheese. They can be eaten from mid- to late spring around to mid- to late summer.

Saving seed The plants have flowers and seeds in all stages of maturity, so you must be ready to gather seeds every few days as they ripen.

Sowing in a seedbed Mid- to late spring through to mid- to late summer – sow a pinch 12 mm (1/2 in) deep, in an 20–25 cm (8–10 in) grid pattern.

Sowing under glass Sow early spring onwards in deep trays/pots in the greenhouse.

Thinning outdoors Thin to the best seedling at each station.

Planting out When the seeds grown under glass are strong enough to handle, plant them in dibbed and puddled holes, 20–25 cm (8–10 in) apart.

Protection Use fleece or fine net to protect from birds, frost, and strong sun. Collect the slugs and snails by hand.

Care Remove yellow leaves and debris and add a mulch to keep down weeds and to hold in moisture.

Cropping Cut the lettuces close to the ground and pick leaves as needed.

Spinach

This is wonderful when picked fresh and eaten raw, and it can be cropped for the best part of the year.

Saving seed To avoid cross-pollination, you must be at least 8 km (5 miles) away from your nearest neighbors. Let the plant mature, flower, and seed, then pull and dry the plant and strip the seeds in an upward motion.

Sowing in raised beds Mid-spring onwards – sow a pinch of seeds about 7.5 cm (3 in) apart.

Thinning outdoors Thin to the best seedling at each station. As the seedlings mature, pick and eat every other plant so as to leave plants 15 cm (6 in) apart.

Protection Use fleece or fine net to protect from birds, frost, and strong sun. Collect the slugs and snails by hand.

Care Remove yellow leaves and debris and add a mulch to keep down weeds and to hold in moisture.

Cropping First crop every other seedling to leave the plants 15 cm (6 in) apart, and finally crop alternate rows.

STALKS AND SHOOTS

Asparagus

There is no denying that asparagus takes time to establish, but once in place it will crop for 20 years or more. Sow and plant in spring, and harvest in years two and three.

Saving seed Although asparagus can be raised from seed, it is much better to start by planting one-year-old crowns. You could save money by asking friends for crowns.

Planting first year Open up a trench about 25 cm (10 in) deep and 38 cm (10 in) wide, and cover the base with well-rotted compost. In the second year, in spring, set the crowns 45 cm (18 in) apart; cover with rotted compost and water generously.

Protection Needs little protection.

Care Remove yellow leaves and debris. Layer mulch around the plants to keep down weeds and hold in moisture. In the first and second years, cut away the foliage just before the berries develop. In the third year, in early spring, draw mulch over the plant.

Cropping In the third year, from mid-spring to early summer, cut the spears when they are 7.5–10 cm (3–4 in) high at a point 7.5–10 cm (3–4 in) below ground.

Celery

For best eating, celery needs to be freshly picked and eaten raw with brown bread. If sown in early to mid-spring and planted on in early summer, it can be cropped from late autumn.

Saving seed To avoid cross-pollination, your garden must be at least 1.5 km (1 mile) from your neighbors. Leave the center of the plant to overwinter, so that it flowers and produces seeds in the following spring. Dry and collect the seeds.

Sowing in peat pots Early to mid-spring – sow a pinch of seeds 12 mm (½ in) deep.

Thinning out When the seedlings are strong enough to handle, thin them out to one strong plant for each pot.

Planting out Set the pots out in a 23 cm (9 in) grid pattern.

Protection Cover with fine net to protect from birds. Remove slugs by hand.

Care As the plant grows, keep adding compost mulch to cover all but the highest leaves.

Cropping Late autumn onwards.

Globe artichokes

Globe artichokes The good thing about globe artichokes is the fact that, because the plant is a perennial, it can be left in the same bed year on year (a bit like rhubarb).

Saving seed As with asparagus and rhubarb, it is best with this plant not to bother with seed but to beg roots/suckers from friends and plant them direct in the bed.

Planting out Set the roots/suckers 10–15 cm (4–6 in) deep in a 45 cm (18 in) grid pattern, say no more than two plants to a 90 cm (3 ft) square bed.

Protection Remove slugs by hand. Stick greenfly and aphids really like artichokes. At the first signs of attack, drench the plants and bed with a liquid soap solution and then clear up and burn the debris.

Care As the plant grows, keep adding compost to blank out the weeds. Keep the bed clean; remove yellow leaves and debris.

Cropping Early autumn onwards.

PODS AND SEEDS

Broad beans

We grow large numbers of broad beans; we eat them fresh and freeze the rest.

Saving seed Let the best plants run to seed and collect and dry the best beans.

Sowing in raised beds Mid-spring or late autumn (depending upon variety) – sow 5–7.5 cm (2–3 in) deep, in a 20 cm (8 in) grid pattern.

Protection Hardy – needs little protection other than support with sticks if you live in a windy area.

Care Remove yellow leaves and debris. Layer mulch around the plants to keep down weeds and hold in moisture, and pinch out the tops when the lower flowers are well formed and set.

Cropping Late summer onwards.

French beans

We only grow French beans to fill the gap before the runner beans.

Saving seed Let the best plants runs to seed and collect and dry the best beans.

Sowing in raised beds Late spring – sow 5–7.5 cm (2–3 in) deep, in a 15 cm (6 in) grid pattern.

Protection Hardy – needs little protection other than support with sticks and string if you live in a windy area.

Care Remove yellow leaves and debris. Layer mulch around the plants to keep down weeds and hold in moisture, and pinch out the tops when the lower flowers are well formed and set.

Cropping Late summer onwards.

Runner beans

We grow and eat as many runner beans as possible – they are fun to grow and they are very tasty. We enjoy them steamed, sprinkled with cheese, and dribbled with mint sauce.

Saving seed Let the best plants run to seed and collect and dry the best beans.

Sowing Late spring to early summer – just to be doubly sure of a crop, we sow both in pots in the greenhouse and directly in the beds.

Planting out Whether planting out or sowing direct, make sure the finished plants finish up about 15–20 cm (6–8 in) apart.

Protection Plants must be protected from slugs, cold weather, and wind. We build a support frame/wigwam from sticks 1.8–2.4 m (6–8 ft) in length. At the early tender stage, we cover the plants with nets to protect from winds and frost.

Care Remove yellow leaves and debris. Layer mulch around the plants to keep down weeds and hold in moisture. Pinch out the tops when the lower flowers are well formed and set. Always be on the lookout for slugs and mice. Water generously.

Cropping Mid-summer onwards.

Peas

Peas are tasty when fresh and almost as tasty frozen. We try to grow a good range of early, mid- and main varieties, so that we can eat them fresh from early summer.

Saving seed Let the best plants run to seed and collect and dry the best peas.

Sowing in the greenhouse As early as possible depending upon variety – sow peas in 90 cm (3 ft) lengths of plastic gutter in the greenhouse, 5–10 cm (2–4 in) apart.

Sowing in raised beds Mid- to late spring – sow about 2.5 cm (1 in) deep, in a 13–15 cm (5–6 in) grid pattern.

Planting out When the greenhouse-grown plants are well developed and the weather is right, take the gutters, make gutter-shaped channels across the bed, about 10–20 cm (4–8 in) apart, and slide the plants into place.

Protection They need to be netted from birds, supported with sticks, and protected from slugs, mice, and rats. We generally set humane mousetraps.

Care Remove yellow leaves and debris. Layer mulch around the plants to keep down weeds and hold in moisture, and pinch out the tops when the lower flowers are well formed and set. Spray with an organic drench if you see signs of white mold or mildew.

Cropping Early summer onwards.

Sweetcorn

We grow as much sweetcorn as possible and eat it boiled, and oiled and barbecued. It is one of those vegetables that most of us enjoy.

Saving seed Sweetcorn can be saved from seed, just like peas and beans. Let the best plants run to seed and collect and dry the best heads.

Sowing in the greenhouse Late spring – sow 2.5–5 cm (1–2 in) deep in peat pots.

Planting out When the plants are strong enough to handle, with stems sturdy, slightly hairy and thick as a pencil, plant them out in the bed on a 30 cm (1 ft) grid pattern, with about nine plants to a 90 cm (3 ft) square bed.

Protection Support with sticks if you live in a windy area, and bank mulch around the plants to give them extra support. Cover the plants with nets if you see signs of bird damage. Use traps if you see mouse damage.

Care Remove yellow leaves and debris. Layer mulch around the plants to keep down weeds and hold in moisture.

Cropping Late summer onwards.

ONIONS AND RELATIVES

Onions and shallots

We eat large numbers of onions in stews, roasts, soups, stir-fries, salads, pickles, and chutneys. We always grow as many as space allows.

Saving seed Sow greenhouse-grown seedlings at least 30 cm (1 ft) apart, choose one or more of the growing onions (best if it is the pick of the crop, hard and firm to the touch, and at least 225 g (8 oz) in weight), stake up the flower stems, and when the flowerheads are black cut them off and dry them in a paper bag.

Sowing in greenhouse Sow very thinly, 6 mm (¼ in) deep, in boxes and water generously. Thin the delicate, grass-like seedlings when they are just big enough to handle.

Planting out in raised beds When the seedlings are no thicker than a pencil, take a clump, trim down off the roots and the tips of the leaves, and set them 2.5 cm (1 in) deep in dibbed holes, in a 7.5–15 cm (3–6 in) grid pattern. Fill the holes and firm the seedlings into place.

Protection Hardy – needs little protection other than to water generously and cover with nets.

Care Remove yellow leaves and debris. Layer mulch around the plants to keep down weeds and hold in moisture.

Cropping As and when the leaves die back and yellow, lift the onions and arrange them so that the roots look to the sun and slowly dry.

Leeks

Leeks are not only tasty and wonderfully easy to grow, but they can be left in place in the beds to overwinter. Last year we were pulling and eating leeks when there was a frost on the ground.

Saving seed Sow your leek seeds as for a normal planting. When you come to harvesting, leave the best specimens about 45 cm (18 in) apart for seed. Leave these plants in place through the second summer. When they are 1.2–1.5 m (4–5 ft) high, support them with stakes. Finally, when the seedheads turn black, put them in paper bags and dry them as for onions.

Sowing in the greenhouse Early to mid-spring (depending upon variety) – sow in boxes in the greenhouse in much the same way as onions. Gradually thin them out to 2.5–5 cm (1–2 in) apart.

Planting out in raised beds In early to mid-spring through to summer, when the seedlings are as thick as a pencil, lift them in bunches, trim off the roots and tips, as for onions, and then drop them singly into 15 cm (6 in) deep dibbed holes. Leave the holes open and water generously.

Protection They need little protection other than to net against birds and squirrels.

Care As the plants grow in size and girth, gradually put mulch around the plants so that all but the tops are covered. Cover with loose dry straw if the weather turns frosty.

Cropping Depending upon variety, pull from early autumn onwards.

Garlic

As we are enthusiastic about the medicinal benefits of garlic, we grow huge amounts and eat it daily. Maybe we are a bit cranky, but then again we don't catch many colds.

Sowing/planting To be doubly sure of a crop we only sow from sets. In autumn or spring (depending upon variety), take single cloves and set them 10–15 cm (4–6 in) deep in a 15–20 cm (6–8 in) grid pattern.

Protection Cover with nets to prevent birds picking at the shoots.

Care Water little and often to prevent bolting.

Cropping When the leaves begin to yellow and die back, gently lift the bulbs with a fork and leave them to dry in the sun.

ROOTS AND TUBERS

Jerusalem artichokes

These are a good option if you enjoy making soups. They are very easy to grow – last year we planted 20 plants and each one gave us a bucket of tubers.

Saving seed Don't bother with seed; it is much better to grow from saved tubers, just like potatoes.

Planting out in raised beds Take the egg-sized tubers and plant them 13–15 cm (5–6 in) deep, in a 23–25 cm (9–10 in) grid pattern.

Protection Needs no protection other than to pick off slugs at the early tender leaf stage.

Care When the shoots are about 30 cm (1 ft) high, cover them with a mound of mulch. If your plot is windy, support the 3–6 m (10–20 ft) high plants with stakes.

Cropping When the flowers and leaves begin to die back, cut the stems down to about 30 cm (1 ft) high. Dig as needed.

Beetroot

Beetroot is easy to grow and store, it is very tasty hot or cold, and it can be made into pickle or chutney.

Saving seed We buy in our seed.

Sowing in raised beds From spring to summer – soak seeds in water for about an hour and then sow them direct in the bed in a small pinch about 2.5 cm (1 in) deep, in a 10–13 cm (4–5 in) grid pattern. When the seedlings are big enough to handle, pinch them out to the best plant.

Protection Remove slugs at the delicate leaf stage.

Care Water generously and put mulch around the plants to hold in the water. Remove yellow leaves and debris.

Cropping When the roots are as big as eggs, lift every other root for tender eating and allow the remaining roots to grow on to full size. Finally lift the roots, twist off the leaves, and eat fresh or store in dry sand.

Carrots

We grow lots of carrots as they are relatively easy to grow, they are easy to store, the old ones seem to get sweeter with age, they taste good hot or cold, and they can be used in all sorts of pickles and chutneys.

Saving seed Sow and grow as usual, but let one or more choice plants grow to seed. Cut the seedheads when they begin to open and spill, and tie them in a paper bag to catch the seed.

Sowing in raised beds Mid- to late spring onwards (depending upon variety) – sow thinly 9 mm (¾ in) deep, with 13–15 cm (5–6 in) between rows. When the seedlings are large enough to handle, thin to about 5 cm (2 in) apart.

Protection Ring with plastic or nets to keep off the carrot fly.

Care Water little and often to prevent bolting. Pull the growing medium up around the tender roots. Remove slugs by hand.

Cropping Lift as needed.

Parsnips

Parsnips can be boiled, roasted, or steamed. They are relatively easy to grow and can be left in the ground over winter.

Saving seed Sow and grow as usual, but let one or more choice plants grow to seed. Cut the seedheads when they begin to open and spill, and tie them in a paper bag to catch the seed.

Sowing in raised beds Mid-spring onwards (according to variety) – sow a pinch of seed 12 mm (½ in) deep, in a 13–15 cm (5–6 in) grid pattern. When large enough to handle, thin to the single best plant at each position.

Protection Pick off slugs at the early tender leaf stage.

Care Add extra mulch to protect the roots and to hold in the water. Remove yellow leaves and debris.

Cropping When the foliage dies back, use a fork to lift as needed.

Potatoes

These are easy to grow in raised beds. There is no denying that shop-bought potatoes are cheap, but they have been sprayed a dozen or so times before you get to eat them. Homegrown potatoes taste so much better.

Saving seed The cheapest and easiest way to get a good low-cost crop of maincrop potatoes is to buy some 'Desiree' potatoes and pick out the egg-sized ones for planting.

Chitting Late winter onwards – set the seed potatoes, rose end uppermost, in trays and leave them in a frost-free shed until the black eyes turn to long, cream-green shoots.

Planting out in raised beds Mid-spring onwards – take the seed potatoes and set them shoots uppermost in 15 cm (6 in) deep holes, in a 30 cm (12 in) grid pattern, so there are about four plants to a 90 cm (3 ft) square bed.

Protection Remove slugs.

Care Every 2–3 weeks, add extra frames and mulch so that all but the top leaves are covered. Remove all yellow leaves and debris.

Cropping Lift early varieties when the flowers are fully open, and all others when the tops have died down.

Radishes

We grow a few crops of radishes in special beds and the rest as fill-ins in odd spaces between other plants. If you sow in succession every two weeks, you will be able to crop from mid-spring through to late winter.

Saving seed Leave the best radishes to flower and seed. When the flowers set to fat pods, wait until the pods start to split and then collect and dry the seed.

Sowing in raised beds From early spring – sow thinly 12 mm (½ in) deep in rows 10–15 cm (4–6 in) apart. When the seedlings are large enough to handle, thin to about 2.5 cm (1 in) apart.

Protection In dry weather, water generously and add extra mulch.

Care Water little and often to prevent bolting. Pull the growing medium up around the tender roots. Remove slugs by hand.

Cropping Pull when needed.

Swedes

A good, relatively easy option if you do not want to grow potatoes. We enjoy them as a meal in themselves, mashed with milk and cream and accompanied by brown bread and butter.

Saving seed It is much better to buy seed.

Sowing in raised beds Late spring – sow a pinch of seed 12 mm (½ in) deep on a 23–25 cm (9–10 in) grid pattern. When the seedlings are strong enough to handle, thin to the best plants.

Protection Pick off slugs at the early tender leaf stage, and cover with nets or fleece to guard against butterflies.

Care If the weather is wet and cold, cover with plastic to shed water and to hold in the heat. If the weather turns icy, protect with dry straw. Remove yellow leaves and debris.

Cropping When the foliage dies back, lift as needed.

Turnips

We grow small, fast-growing varieties as a catch crop between slow-growing vegetables. You can eat them in stews and sliced in stir-fries.

Saving seed Sow and grow as usual, and let one or more choice plants grow to seed. Cut the seedheads when they begin to open and spill, and tie them in a paper bag to catch the seed.

Sowing in raised beds Early summer onwards – sow a pinch of seed 12 mm (½ in) deep, in a 15–20 cm (6–8 in) grid pattern. When the seedlings are big enough to handle, thin them to the best plants.

Protection Remove slugs at the delicate leaf stage.

Care Water generously and put mulch around the plants to hold in water. Remove yellow leaves and debris. Cover with fleece to guard against butterflies.

Cropping Harvest young leaves to eat as greens, and then from mid-autumn onwards lift as needed.

Celeriac

We mainly eat celeriac fine-chopped in cut winter salads, as we enjoy the nutty taste and texture – a bit like a fresh celery heart.

Saving seed It is best to buy seed.

Sowing under glass Early to mid-spring – sow thinly in boxes and then transplant the seedlings into pots.

Planting out in raised beds In mid-spring, leave the pots out for a day or two and then plant the sturdy seedlings out in the beds in a 7.5 cm (3 in) grid pattern.

Protection Add extra mulch to give support and to hold in moisture.

Care Cut off straggly sideshoots and draw the mulch up if the weather turns cold. Remove yellow leaves and debris. Remove slugs by hand.

Cropping When the foliage has died back, cover the bed with straw or fleece and lift as needed.

FRUITING VEGETABLES

Aubergines (eggplants)

We grow aubergines because their shape, texture and color is extraordinary and because we like to cook them with courgettes (zucchini).

Saving seed Cut a ripe aubergine into small pieces and squeeze and mash them by hand. Rinse the resultant mess in water, and catch the seeds in a cotton cloth or fine sieve. Repeat the process and dry the resultant seeds until you have enough for your needs.

Sowing in a greenhouse Early spring – sow the seeds in a shallow box and cover with newspaper and glass. When the seedlings are big enough to handle, transplant them into pots.

Planting out in raised beds When the seedlings are sturdy and the weather is frost free, plant the seedlings out, with 2–3 plants to a 90 cm (3 ft) square bed.

Protection Support with stakes and build a plastic or net screen on the windward side.

Care Remove weak/unwanted flowers and fruit so as to keep 5–6 of the best examples. Spread extra mulch to hold in moisture.

Cropping When the fruits are plump and well colored, cut them off with a sharp knife.

Capsicums (sweet peppers)

Sweet peppers are not only fun to grow in much the same way as tomatoes and aubergines (eggplants), but they can be used hot or cold in a whole range of meals. Gill and I make chutney from onions, apples, tomatoes, and sweet peppers – very tasty!

Saving seed Cut open the ripe pepper and collect and dry the seed.

Sowing in a greenhouse Early spring – sow the seeds in a shallow box and cover with newspaper and glass. When the seedlings are big enough to handle, transplant them into pots.

Planting out in raised beds When the seedlings are sturdy and the weather is frost free, plant the seedlings into the bed, with about two plants to a 90 cm (3 ft) square bed.

Protection Support with stakes and build a plastic screen on the windward side.

Care Remove weak/unwanted flowers and fruit so as to keep 5–6 of the best examples. Spread extra mulch to hold in moisture.

Cropping Cut off with a sharp knife when the fruits are plump and colored to your liking – young and green or mature and red.

Cucumbers (outdoor ridge type)

If you have only ever tasted the ordinary greenhouse-grown cucumbers, then you are going to be in for a big surprise. Ridge-type cucumbers not only have a good strong taste and texture, but they can be pickled and turned into gherkins.

Saving seed Cut and mash the ripe fruits and wash, sieve, and dry the seed.

Sowing in a greenhouse Early to mid-spring – sow two seeds 18 mm (¾ in) deep in peat pots and cover with newspaper and glass. Thin to the best plants.

Planting out in raised beds When the seedlings are sturdy with hairy stems, plant them out, with a single plant to a 90 cm (3 ft) square bed.

Protection Use sticks or plastic pipe and fleece to give protection against both winds and frost.

Care Pinch out the ends of the growing tips after 5–6 true leaves have been produced. Spread extra mulch to hold in moisture. If necessary, add an extra frame so that you can spread a greater depth of mulch. Keep removing slugs by hand.

Cropping Cut off with a sharp knife when the fruits are small plump and firm. Keep picking to encourage more growth.

Marrows and courgettes (zucchini)

There are many kinds of marrows and courgettes (zucchini), which are all tasty. To be doubly sure of a crop, start them off in the greenhouse and plant more than you need.

Saving seed Cut open the ripe fruit, mash the lumps, and then wash and sieve the mess. Collect and dry the seed.

Sowing in a greenhouse Early spring – sow two seeds, 18 mm (¾ in) deep, per peat pot, and cover with newspaper and glass. When the seedlings are big enough to handle, thin them to the best plants.

Planting out in raised beds When the seedlings are sturdy with hairy stems, and the weather is frost free, plant the seedlings in the bed, with no more than two plants to a 90 cm (3 ft) square bed.

Protection Support with stakes or plastic pipe, and cover with fleece, net, or plastic sheet to protect against winds and frosts.

Care Remove slugs by hand and spread extra mulch to hold in moisture.

Cropping Cut off with a sharp knife when the fruits are plump and the correct size. Keep cropping to encourage growth.

Tomatoes

We are not keen on freshly picked tomatoes, but we add them to a courgette (zucchini), onion, and aubergine (eggplant) mix that we freeze for the winter, and to various stir-fries; we also turn tomatoes into chutneys and sauces.

Saving seed Cut the ripe tomatoes into pieces, pulp with your hands, and then wash and sieve the resultant mess. Dry the seed and save in paper bags.

Sowing in a greenhouse Early spring – sow the seeds in a shallow box and cover with newspaper and glass. When the seedlings are big enough to handle, transplant them into peat pots.

Planting out in raised beds When the seedlings are sturdy with hairy stems and the weather is frost free, plant them out, with 2–3 plants to a 90 cm (3 ft) square bed.

Protection Support with stakes and build a plastic screen on the windward side.

Care Support with ties every 30 cm (1 ft) as the plant grows in height. Remove sideshoots. When the plants are about 4–6 trusses high, according to type and vigor, then pinch out the topmost shoots to halt the growth. Spread extra mulch to hold in moisture. Remove yellow leaves and debris.

Cropping Snap the fruit off at the knuckle when the tomatoes are small, well colored, plump, and firm.

HERBS

In many ways, herbs are an essential part of shoestring self-sufficiency. This is not to say that without them all your efforts would count for nought – as, for example, you could not manage without heating, lighting, or fresh water – but rather that without them your self-sufficient life would be much poorer. Just as birdsong and dappled sunlight lift our spirits and help us through the difficult times, so it is with herbs. For example, when Gill was putting together a meal of locally caught fish with our own freshly gathered runner beans and peas, I picked a handful of fresh mint and swiftly created a sauce made from chopped mint, cider vinegar, brown sugar, and honey. Certainly, it was a beautiful meal in its own right, but there was no doubt that everything about the meal was heightened by the addition of the mint sauce.

If all that sounds a bit purple and arty-poetical, well maybe it is. The fact is that if you take a whole year's worth of hot and cold meals, snacks, preserves, pickles, chutneys, drinks, and so on – hot soups and stews in winter, teas and tisanes for colds and sore throats, refreshing salads, roast meats – and add carefully chosen fresh herbs to the equation, then you can see that in some sense they are essential. To put it another way, if we take it as read that all our self-sufficient efforts are powered by good, fresh, organic food, we could say that if food is the energy that powers our self-sufficient lifestyle then herbs are the lubrication that oils the wheels.

Shoestring herbs

In the context of shoestring self-sufficiency, herbs are all-round winners. When we moved to this house, our neighbor called round and gave us a lot of roots, cuttings, and seeds from her herb garden – 20 or so plants, everything from bay through to rosemary and many more besides. Many years later, all these herbs are still growing strong. Some plants, like mint, just keep rooting year in year out, and others we keep going by saving seed, but the fact is that the whole collection has not cost us a single penny. I am sure that Henry David Thoreau would have approved. My advice is to start with familiar items that you want quickly, and then try less familiar herbs when time allows.

Bay (sweet bay)
* Description – hardy evergreen shrub with aromatic leaves
* Height – 1.8–3.5 m (6–12 ft)
* Position – well-drained, moist, sunny
* Herbal – for nerves, eyes and bruises
* Cooking – we use it to flavor stews and fish

Borage
* Description – hardy annual with hairy green leaves
* Height – about 90 cm (3 ft)
* Position – well-drained, moist, sunny
* Herbal – to increase perspiration, as a mild sedative, and as a wash for soothing skin
* Cooking – we use it in cold drinks and salads

Chervil
* Description – hardy biennial, usually grown as an annual, with bright green, fern-like leaves, looks like parsley
* Height – about 45 cm (18 in)
* Position – rich, moist, sunny
* Herbal – Culpeper's *Herbal* says good for bruises and swellings
* Cooking – we use the delicate aniseed-flavored leaves in salads and sandwiches, and in fish and egg dishes

Chives
* Description – hardy perennial with green tubular stems topped with round, rose-pink flowerheads
* Height – about 30 cm (1 ft)
* Position – well-watered, sheltered, sunny corner
* Herbal – used traditionally to stimulate the appetite and as a cold cure
* Cooking – we use the distinctive onion-like stems and leaves in sandwiches and omelets

Dill
* Description – hardy annual with tall stems topped with feathery blue-green leaves
* Height – 60–90 cm (2–3 ft)
* Position – well-drained, fertile, sheltered, sunny
* Herbal – Culpeper's *Herbal* says good for curing wind, easing pain, and encouraging rest
* Cooking – we use the freshly picked leaves to garnish and flavor new potatoes and white fish

Fennel
* Description – hardy herbaceous perennial with tall stems, feathery green leaves, and golden-yellow flowerheads
* Height – 1.5–1.8 m (5–6 ft)
* Position – moist, well-drained, fertile, sheltered, sunny
* Herbal – Culpeper's *Herbal* says good as a rub for cramps, as an aromatic for wheezing, and as a wash for tired eyes
* Cooking – we use the leaves with fish, salads, stews, cakes, and bread

Mint (common)
* Description – hardy herbaceous perennial with mid-green leaves
* Height – about 60 cm (2 ft)
* Position – moisture-retentive, fertile, warm, sheltered
* Herbal – used traditionally by herbalists as a cure for sore skin, for clearing the head, and as a rub to help with scurf and dandruff
* Cooking – we use the leaves chopped with brown sugar and mixed with vinegar and honey to make mint sauce, and we add the picked leaves to boiled new potatoes

Parsley
* Description – hardy biennial usually grown as an annual, with curly, tight-packed green leaves
* Height – 20–25 cm (8–12 in)
* Position – moisture-retentive, fertile, sun or shade
* Herbal – Culpeper's *Herbal* says good for earache and as a wash for swollen eyes
* Cooking – we use the leaves in sauces and as a garnish

Rosemary
* Description – evergreen shrub with narrow, spiky, dark green, aromatic leaves
* Height – 90 cm (3 ft) plus
* Position – just about anywhere
* Herbal – we always have a bunch of rosemary hanging at the head of the bed – we like the scent and find it relaxing
* Cooking – we use the leaves to flavor fish and meat dishes

Sage
* Description – hardy evergreen shrub with long, aromatic, green-grey leaves
* Height 60–90 cm (2–3 ft)
* Position – fertile, warm, sheltered
* Herbal – my grandmother used to chop the leaves and mix them with apple cider vinegar and honey to ease a sick headache and sore throat
* Cooking – we use the leaves in sage and onion stuffing, cheese dips, and nut roasts

Thyme
* Description – hardy dwarf evergreen shrub with small, aromatic leaves
* Height – 10–30 cm (4–12 in)
* Position – light, well-drained, airy, sunny
* Herbal – traditionally thyme is used for curing just about everything from warts and swellings through to wind and joint aches
* Cooking – we use the leaves with fish and rich wild meats like hare and rabbit

SOFT FRUIT
AND TREE FRUIT

Rhubarb

Our few beds of rhubarb must surely be the ultimate in shoestring food. We eat it stewed with apples, we make it into crumbles, we add it to various other fruits to make jam, and we sell it at the gate. A good way forward if you are planting afresh is to beg half a dozen roots from neighbors, plant them in various places around the garden, and then use the ones that do best in your particular location.

Protection If a deep frost is forecast, cover the beds with a thick layer of straw topped with plastic sheet.

Care Remove yellow leaves and debris. Sometime towards the end of the growing season add a mulch of horse manure. If you want to try for an early crop, cover selected shoots with something like an old bucket or box so that the shoots are in the dark.

Cropping Select a good-looking stalk, grip it firmly, and pull it free. Using a sharp knife, slash off the ends, and put them on the compost heap.

Blackberries

When we first came here, we planted blackberries in rows against wires and along one boundary as a hedge. Now everywhere we look our patch is fringed and dotted with blackberry bushes. We eat them fresh or cooked with apples, and we turn them into wine; they can also be frozen. The best thing, however, and this is why we are letting them run a bit wild, is that our bees love them. One moment the bees are buzzing around the blackberries, and the next we are harvesting honey – to eat, give to friends, and sell at the gate. A good shoestring option, if you are short of ground, is not to grow blackberries but to forage for wild ones.

Protection We don't do anything to our blackberries except slash them back when they start moving towards the house.

Care Every now and then, we cut selected bushes down to the ground and burn the debris, so that the bushes grow afresh and are invigorated.

Cropping When the time for blackberry picking comes around, we take baskets and sandwiches and make it into a picnic event. It reminds us of when we were children.

Currants

We grow all the currants – red to turn into jelly, and black and white to turn into jam and pies. The easiest way of starting out is to beg roots from friends. Be mindful that, while all the currants look much the same, blackcurrants need to be treated slightly different from red and white.

Protection Cover the bushes once the fruit starts to form. We cover them in tents made from old net curtains held together with washing pegs and bits of string – not very pretty, but it does the trick.

Care After planting blackcurrants, cut the stems down to about 2.5 cm (1 in) above the ground. From then on, only prune out the shoots that have fruited. After planting red and white currants, cut the main shoots back by half, and then in late winter cut out any shoots that crowd the center.

Cropping Strip the berries as soon as they are ready. We take off what we need in one large harvest and then remove the nets and let the birds have the rest.

Gooseberries

In our garden we have three bushes that, we have been told, have been in place since just about 1911. Could it really be that they are a hundred years old? All we know for sure is that they are at least 20 years old and they give us as much golden fruit as we can take. We eat them in pies, in crumbles, and best of all in jam. In the context of shoestring self-sufficiency, gooseberries give wonderful value.

Protection In our experience gooseberries need little protection. All we do is drape them with nets when they are fruiting and make sure they are fenced against rabbits.

Care After planting, cut back the main branches by half and then in the following autumn cut back all the shoots that formed in that year. From then on, at the end of the season cut the season's growth back by half and clear out the center of the bush.

Cropping Our bushes are a mass of thorns, so we always pick the fruit slowly and with great care.

Raspberries

We have a single long bed of raspberries – half summer-fruiting and half autumn-fruiting. We tend to eat them fresh, make some into jam, and then freeze the rest. Gill is a very keen raspberry eater. I like them in jam and straight out of the freezer – so that they are ice bound – and covered with homemade yogurt.

Protection Birds can be a real nuisance. When the plants are fruiting, we drape them with nets to keep off the birds and squirrels.

Care If you see signs of aphids (lots of sticky mess and curling leaves), spray them with an organic wash and then remove and burn the debris. At the end of the season, cut autumn-fruiting varieties down to the ground. With summer-fruiting varieties, in spring when the canes start to grow cut all the old canes down to ground level and tie up all the new growth.

Cropping Pick them on the day of eating, or pick and freeze as soon as possible.

Strawberries

Strawberries must surely be one of the best all-time shoestring winners. I say this because not only do our gifted plants give us a huge amount of fruit – for example, last year the plants produced more than we could eat fresh, give away, and freeze – but the plants, year after year, produce little runners or new plants that we use to make new plants, give away, and sell on.

Protection Strawberries need lots of protection from birds, mice, and slugs. We cover with nets, put traps down for the mice, and remove slugs by hand.

Care Remove yellow leaves and debris, put down a mulch of dry straw, and water generously in dry weather.

Cropping Start picking the moment the fruit is plump and well colored – then keep cropping to keep the fruit coming.

Apples

We have a dozen or so apple trees, including a range of eating and dessert varieties. Apples are important to us for eating in the hand, for cooking, for freezing, for cider making, and of course for the blossom for the bees. Make sure when you are setting up new trees that you get the best varieties that are recommended for your area.

Protection The best protection is to make sure that the new planted trees are well staked, and from then on keep the trees clean and well pruned. We encourage our geese to feed in the orchard so that they manure the ground and eat the various bug and beetle pests.

Care A good single tip if you don't know about pruning is to cut the wood away from the center of the tree, so the overall tree shape looks a bit like an umbrella; branches and foliage should look down rather than up.

Cropping Our varieties were chosen for their character and type and for the fact that their fruit is ready at different times, so that we have a long fruiting season.

Pears

We are lucky in that when we came here there were already six or so mature pear trees. Be aware when you are choosing trees that there are any number of varieties and sizes. Good advice if you are starting out is to go to a specialist and tell them your ambitions and needs.

Protection We do nothing much at all to protect our trees other than to remove and burn the debris, and generally shape the trees so that the fruit is easy to reach.

Care I was told by an old country gaffer that the best way of caring for a pear tree was, at the end of the season, to use water with the addition of a little paraffin, and a stiff brush, to wash as much of the tree as we could reach, especially the trunk. It works for us.

Cropping Pick the fruit with care – no dropping or bruising.

Plums

We have three types of plum – Victoria, greengage, and damson. They are all beautiful. We eat them fresh, in tarts and crumbles, cooked with yogurt or custard, and mixed with apples in jam. We enjoy them, the kids love them, the geese cannot get enough of them, and of course the bees really do well from the blossom.

Protection Apart from allowing the geese to clean up the ground around the trees, and the annual collecting and burning of the debris (leaves, twigs, moldy fruit), we pretty much leave our trees untouched.

Care A good rule of thumb with plum trees is to keep them shaped so that all the fruit is within reach. If nothing else, wait until the fruit has been picked and then cut back the wood from the center of the tree.

Cropping Pick the fruit the very moment that it is ripe, firm, and well colored. When there is a glut, we eat it fresh, make lots of jam, and sell the rest at the gate.

STORING AND PRESERVING FOOD

In the context of this book, storing and preserving food involves saving, laying up, or squirreling away all the foods that you have grown, and all the foods that you have exchanged, been given, purchased as gluts from farmers' markets, foraged, and/or otherwise produced – meaning foods like meat, eggs, fish, and honey. Storing and preserving food is central to the practice and philosophy of shoestring self-sufficiency.

For Gill and me, the act of storing and preserving food not only makes us feel as if we are doing our bit for the common greater good, but it also makes us feel self-reliant, strong, and enriched – as if we are pioneers or homesteaders battling against the elements.

Storing and preserving homegrown produce is a winner on many counts: it is cheaper than shop-bought food, it is certainly tastier, and most importantly we know exactly what it contains. For example, we have just eaten cookies that we made from locally grown oats and butter and our own honey and goose eggs, and they were delicious – no fancy packaging, no transporting exotic ingredients halfway around the world, and no strange chemicals included just to enhance taste and extend shelf life.

Preserved and stored food

Food preservation and storing is the process of treating and handling food to stop or slow down spoilage – or you might simply say it is a way of making food last longer. Preservation and storage usually involves preventing the growth of bacteria, yeasts, and molds and/or putting the food through a process that slows down visual deterioration. Many processes designed to preserve food involve a number of different methods. Preserving fruit, by turning it into jam, for example, involves boiling to reduce the fruit's moisture content and to kill bacteria, sugaring to prevent the regrowth of bacteria, and sealing within an airtight jar to prevent recontamination.

There are many traditional methods of preserving or storing food that limit energy input and reduce the carbon footprint. Although for the main part maintaining texture and flavor is an important aspect of food preservation, there are methods that completely change the character of the food being preserved, to the extent that it becomes a product in its own right. For example, when apples, onions, runner beans, sugar, honey, and vinegar are boiled and simmered together, they turn from crisp fruit and vegetables into a delicious golden brown sludge that we call chutney.

Left in the ground There are some vegetables – for example, parsnips, swedes and leeks – that can simply be left in the ground until they are needed. With our leeks, if the weather turns icy cold we cover the bed with a generous layer of dry straw.

Clamping Clamping is a method of storing piles of root crops. The crops are heaped on dry ground and then covered with straw and earth.

Drying Basic air-drying is a method of calling a halt to all the bugs and beasts that require moisture. For example, onions can simply be dried in the sun and then strung up in a cool, dry shed. Take a loop of string, about 45 cm (18 in) long when pulled tight, and hang it up with a small weight at the bottom end. Starting at the bottom, take an onion and tuck the stalk through the double string so that the stalk is gripped in place. Continue until the whole length of the string is tightly packed with onions.

Freezing Freezing is a great way of storing or preserving food. We freeze fruit like raspberries, apple pulp, runner beans, broad beans, messes made from onions, peppers, courgettes (zucchini) and aubergines (eggplants), rabbits, eggs, and fish. Vegetables are dunked into boiling water and then frozen, while meat is frozen as is.

Salting Traditional salting is a method of drying fish, meat and vegetables. Occasionally, we salt belly of pork to make bacon so that we can give it to friends. To do this, clean the pork, rub a small amount of saltpeter into the underside and any bloody areas, and put the pork into a plastic/wooden container and cover it with salt. Pour off the liquid and then repeatedly repeat the salting until the pork become rock hard and dry. Finally, sew the pork into a cotton cloth and hang it up in an airy, cool room to dry. To eat it, simply cut off a thin slice and fry it – it is very tasty.

Bottling We bottle apple pulp, plums, and pears. The produce is prepared, packed into heavy-duty glass jars or bottles, the syrup or water (according to the recipe) is poured into the jars, the whole thing is heated, and finally the jars are capped.

Pickles and chutneys Pickles are items like onions stored whole in vinegar, while chutney is basically a mix of vegetables, vinegar, and sugar that is boiled to a pulp and then bottled.

Jams and jellies Jam is made by boiling and bottling a mix of fruit and sugar. It is a perfect way of storing fruit.

Butter and cheese The best way of dealing with surplus milk is either to feed it to pigs or calves or to turn it into butter or cheese.

Fermenting Most of us know about fermenting – one moment we have apples or blackberries and the next we have cider and wine. We turn all our apples into cider, which is a wonderful drink. Making cider is a great shoestring option. We mash the apples, then squeeze off and bottle the juice – nothing is added or taken away.

HOMEMADE WINE

Homemade country wine is all pleasure: first when foraging for the correct ingredients, then when watching, waiting, and wondering how the wine is going to turn out, and finally, of course, in the drinking. Winemaking is the perfect shoestring self-sufficient activity. You start with a few basics – equipment and ingredients – and then a few months later you have a beautiful bottle of wine. If you think that wine can only be made from fruits like gooseberries, damsons, and elderberries, think again. Wine can be made from fruit, vegetables, and herbs, and just about any plant material – fruit, flowers, leaves, roots – can be turned into wine.

Foraging

Gathering ingredients for free from hedgerows, fields, and woods is great fun in itself. All you do is kit yourself out with a hat, a long walking stick for hooking plants, a generous packed lunch, and plenty of plastic bags, and then off you go. Choose a bit of local countryside – well away from polluted roads and forbidden areas – and then simply collect the known berries, crab apples, or whatever you choose. We particularly like blackberries, elderberries, and crab apples.

WARNING: you must identify all foraged material as being safe – clean, sound, non-poisonous, and free from pollutants.

Equipment

* Mashing container – wood or plastic (not metal) lidded bucket/tub, for the preparation of mixtures of fruit, vegetables, or flowers.
* Sterilizing solution – from a winemaking supplier.
* Fermenting glass/plastic demijohns with a rubber bung and proprietary airlock or 'bubbler' to fit (one demijohn with bung and airlock for each gallon/4.5 liters of wine that you want to make).

Traditional elderberry wine recipe

Purple-black berries (*Sambucus nigra*) that hang in hand-sized bunches on reddish stems and are usually to be found in late summer or early autumn.

* 1.6 kg (3½ lb) elderberries
* 450 g (1 lb) mixed raisins and sultanas, chopped
* 4.5 liters (1 gallon) boiling water
* Juice of 1 lemon
* Yeast (according to manufacturer's instructions)
* 1.3 kg (3 lb) sugar

Method

1 Strip the elderberries from their stems and mash them in a fermenting bin together with the dried fruit.
2 Pour the boiling water over the resultant mess and allow to cool.
3 When the mixture is just cool enough to touch, add the lemon juice and yeast, cover with a lid or cloth and stand in a warm place to ferment.
4 Stir the mix once or twice daily.
5 After seven days, strain off the solids, add the sugar, and stir to dissolve.
6 Transfer the resultant slightly thick liquid to a sterilized demijohn, fit the airlock, and leave in a warm, dark place.
7 When the fermentation has ceased (it has stopped bubbling), transfer the liquid into another sterilized demijohn and fit a bung and airlock.
8 Leave in a cool, dark place for six months, then bottle, cork, and label.
9 Store for a further six months and then have a sip!

BEEKEEPING

Beekeeping is a uniquely exciting and challenging adventure. It is quite unlike any other activity that you can ever imagine – there are so many aspects and possibilities. For example, there are the physical hands-on issues of the beehives – buying them, building them, setting them up, maintenance. There are the bees – their life cycle, the possibility that they might swarm, and their health. Then of course there is the honey – how to get it out of the hive, put it into bottles, and so on. If you are anxious about being a beginner, don't be. When Gill and I first started beekeeping, our biggest problem was not that we were beginners but rather that we were weighed down with mountains of advice and confusing preconceptions.

There is money in honey

The good news is that honey and all the by-products sell well at the gate. Last year we kept back enough honey for friends and family and then sold all the rest. Beekeeping is very different from keeping sheep, cows, or other livestock. You don't need to go to the trouble and expense of building fences or buying in machinery, and you don't have to worry about your stock straying. With bees, you will find that not only will your farming neighbors welcome your bees, but some – like our local apple growers – will pay you to keep them on their land.

Getting started

When we first started, we were unlucky in that we obtained one lot of bees that were overpriced and disease ridden, but conversely very lucky in that we got our other bees from a real old-time honest expert. At the time I felt bad at being cheated by the rogue, but now I understand that by seeing the best bees set directly against the worst – observing the two colonies and comparing notes about health, growth, and honey production – we learned a lot in a short space of time. Better yet the honest expert was so concerned and helpful that along the way he has become a friend and mentor. In that first year, our single good colony gave us over 45 kg (100 lb) of honey and is still doing wonderfully well, while the sickly colony gave us nil honey and is still giving us problems. So where to start? You could search out the beekeepers in your local area, join a society or group, and then maybe see if you can watch and help before buying a colony; or you could, like us, do the reading and the research, make links with a single expert and then make the leap. Get your bees from a recommended, small, local, keen, amateur supplier – someone who is ready to help and advise. Beware of the many large, much-advertised commercial set-ups who are only in it for the money. Be wary of bee-selling adverts that use words such as 'easy' and 'easy money business opportunities.'

The traditional hive

The familiar square box-type hive is layered, a bit like a high-rise tower block. From bottom to top, there is a stand with four legs, an open wire mesh floor with a under-sliding door, a brood or nest chamber that contains frames of wax in which the queen lays eggs, a queen excluder that prevents the queen bee from leaving the brood chamber, one or more 'supers' or honey stores that contain frames of wax in which the worker bees store their excess honey, a crown board, and a roof. Designs of shutters, gates, shelves, and so on vary from hive to hive. A typical beehive is a complex and expensive item.

The bees in action

Within the hive there are three types of bee – a single female queen, 200–300 male drones, and 50,000-plus neuter or undeveloped female workers. Within this set-up, the drones fertilize the queen, the queen lays eggs, and the workers do all the business of carrying water, gathering pollen, collecting nectar, and so on. Through the year the workers forage for nectar and bring it back to the hive, where they store it first in the brood box and then in the supers or honey boxes. In the context of this book, the object of beekeeping is twofold: it is to collect honey and it is to increase food garden yield by having the bees do the pollinating.

The shoestring top bar hive

A typical top bar hive is no more than a long, wooden, trough-shaped box made from 2.5 cm (1 in) thick, rough-sawn wood (see page 130). It is about 1.2 m (4 ft) long, 38 cm (15 in) wide at the top, 20 cm (8 in) wide at the base, and about 30 cm (1 ft) in total depth. The 24 top bars that bridge the 38 cm (15 in) width are about 3.5 cm (1½ in) wide and 2.5 cm (1 in) thick. Running along the center of the underside of each bar – along the length and on the 3.5 cm (1½ in) wide face – is a wide saw slot filled with molten wax. On one 1.2 m (4 ft) side face of the box are five 2.5 cm (1 in) diameter drilled entrance holes. A horizontal top bar beehive of this character can be swiftly made at about a 20th of the cost of a traditional vertical hive. If you want to go extreme shoestring, you could easily make the top bar hive from salvaged wood.

The clothes and equipment

As a beginner, and to give you confidence, you will need an all-in-one suit complete with veil, plus a pair of leather gloves that come complete with canvas gauntlet sleeves. You could reduce the cost by using an old boiler-type suit and only buying the veil and gloves. You will also need a smoker. Light a screw of newspaper, drop it in the smoker, and top it up with wood shavings. Then put on the suit, followed by boots and gloves. Gill checks me over to make sure everything is tucked in and zipped up and then I am off.

Introducing the bees

If you have a traditional beehive, you simply take the frames of bees as purchased and slide them into the center of the brood chamber. If, on the other hand, you have made a top bar hive, as illustrated on page 130, take a frame of bees as purchased, use a pair of secateurs to cut the comb from its wooden frame, and then, with a helper, take a large bodkin and twine and loosely sew the top edge of the comb to the one of the top bars. Continue with the other five or so frames. Don't worry if it all looks a bit wobbly, because the bees will swiftly rebuild and repair the combs to their liking – at which point you can cut away the string.

Harvesting the honey

In a traditional hive, the moment the brood chamber looks a bit crowded you should top the brood chamber with a super or honey box, and then another and another until the end of the season. When the season is over and all the excess honey is stored in the honey boxes, you then take off the frames and use a hand-turned extractor to spin out the honey. In a top bar hive, you simply remove a comb of capped honey, cut the comb from the top bar, and then chop the comb into chunks and eat it as it is. No equipment more expensive than a sharp knife is required.

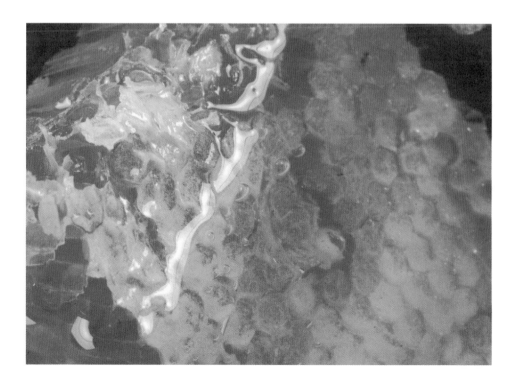

PLANS FOR A TOP BAR HIVE

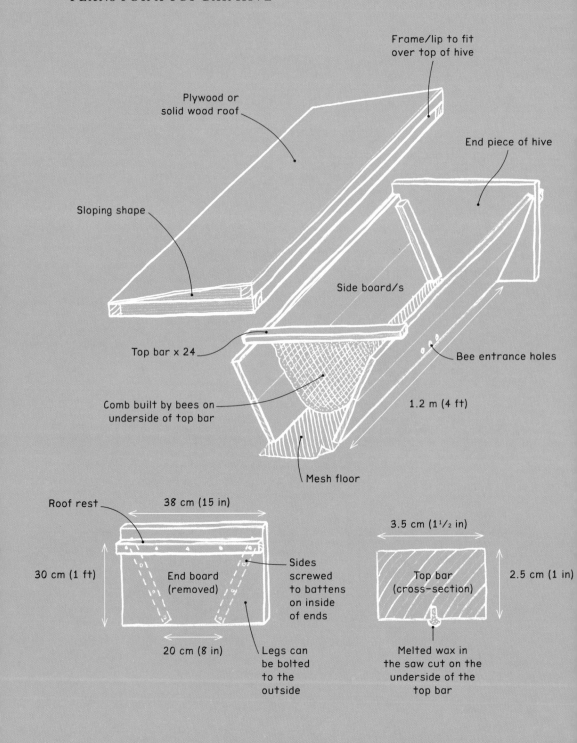

Frame/lip to fit over top of hive

End piece of hive

Plywood or solid wood roof

Sloping shape

Side board/s

Top bar x 24

Bee entrance holes

1.2 m (4 ft)

Comb built by bees on underside of top bar

Mesh floor

Roof rest

38 cm (15 in)

3.5 cm (1½ in)

30 cm (1 ft)

End board (removed)

Sides screwed to battens on inside of ends

Top bar (cross-section)

2.5 cm (1 in)

20 cm (8 in)

Legs can be bolted to the outside

Melted wax in the saw cut on the underside of the top bar

BEEKEEPING CALENDAR FOR A TRADITIONAL HIVE

As some seasons are out of kilter, look at the target season plus the ones either side of the one you are in. Note that you will have to adjust this management plan to suit your hives and the area in which you live.

Mid-winter
* Repair the hives, clothes and all the other hardware.
* Make armchair plans for the coming year.
* Order jars and labels.
* Get a year diary to record events and state of play.

Late winter
* Every week make a judgment about how much honey there is within the hives – do this by giving each hive a lift.
* If you have worries about food, then lightly smoke the bees and remove the crown board. If you see capped stores on several frames, then rest easy.
* Bees bringing in pollen indicates a laying queen.
* An absence of pollen indicates a failing or failed queen.
* Half cover feedholes towards the end of the season.

Early spring
* On warm days there should be plenty of activity.
* Brood rearing will be on the move – check that the colonies have enough food.
* If food stores are low or empty, feed thick syrup.
* Remove mouse guards.
* Save your inspections for warm, sunny days.

Mid-spring
* Be aware that this season is the most variable, with bees variously needing feeding or supering.
* Be aware that good or bad weather can make all the difference to the wellbeing of the colony.
* Choose a warm day to do the spring-cleaning.

* Assess the wellbeing of the colony.
* Mark poor combs so you can deal with them during the season.
* Add supers.
* Set up a spare hive.

Late spring
* Continue seven-day inspections.
* Keep supering in advance of requirements.

Early summer
* If the bees are visiting oil seed rape, swiftly extract honey so as to avoid granulation in the combs.
* Replace wet supers at dusk.
* Continue with regular inspections.
* Be aware that if you have taken stores off prolific bees there might be a shortage of food in the brood chamber.
* Be aware that poor weather could mean that the bees are starving – feed if necessary.

Mid-summer
* Continue making regular inspections.
* Add supers if necessary.
* Think about replacing poor queens.

Late summer
* Nectar income will slow down.
* Close down hive entrances early in the season to prevent robbing by other bees and wasps.
* Extract honey towards the end of the season.
* Check the amount of food in the brood chamber and feed if needed.
* Make sure that all queens are good enough to carry the colonies through the winter.
* Consider varroa treatments after super removal.

Early autumn
* Continue feeding.
* Make sure the queens are not crowded out.
* Super if there is a late flow.
* Unite weak colonies, or those with failing queens.

Mid-autumn
* Finish feeding.
* Check on winter stores.
* Fit mouse guards.
* Uncover the crown board hole to give through ventilation.
* Remove all the vegetation from around the hives.
* Check that the roof is sound.
* Have a final inspection to make sure the queen is still laying worker brood.

Late autumn
* Be aware that this is the first of the quiet seasons.
* Every six weeks or so, make a judgment about the stores within the hives.
* Be aware that prolific bees – the ones that breed throughout the winter – can eat up a lot of food.
* Secure the hives with straps.
* Be aware that bees will fly quite strongly on warmer days.
* If you are concerned about the bees' welfare, remove the hive roof and put your ear to the feedhole or listen in with a stethoscope and tap on the crown board. A short 'roar' is good, but a continual 'moaning' indicates queenlessness.

Early winter
* Follow through as for late autumn.
* Check throughout the season for varroa.
* Think about keeping varroa levels down by puffing icing sugar.
* Read up on the life cycles of queens and workers, swarming, disease recognition and prevention, and all other aspects of beekeeping so that you are well prepared for the year to come.

KEEPING CHICKENS

The way it was

In the late 1950s, when I was a small kid staying with my grandparents in the country, everyone kept chickens. My grandparents and the two old ladies next door had between them about 0.4 hectare (1 acre) for chickens, all housed in two 9 m (30 ft) long sheds, with each shed having 20 or so nesting boxes. To service this set-up, they had several huge galvanized bins full of feed, a small mountain of crushed oyster shell for grit, a barn full of straw bales for bedding, bits and pieces like colored leg rings, feed buckets, water pumps, and rat traps, and lots of wheelbarrows and trolleys. At sunrise, my job was first to let the chickens out into their runs, and then to walk through the sheds with a wicker basket trolley collecting the eggs. As I remember, the sheds were full of dry straw, nose-tickling smells, old hessian sacks nailed up at the windows, and swirling, sunlit dust. When my early morning job was done, I would go back to the kitchen and have a massive breakfast of fried eggs, with honey on toast and tea on the side.

Chickens and shoestring self-sufficiency

Keeping chickens and shoestring self-sufficiency make a perfect eco circle. You have fresh eggs and the pleasure of keeping livestock, the chickens live out their lives in the fresh air, all your kitchen and vegetable garden scraps are fed to the chickens, the chickens occasionally get to wander through the garden so that they can eat all the caterpillars and pests, and at the end of it all your vegetable beds are enriched with as much chicken manure as they can take.

Eggs and meat

Right from the start you need to ask yourself whether you want the meat as well as the eggs. I say this because lot of beginners, especially ones with children, have trouble coming to terms with the facts of life of meat and chickens. The truth is that if you want to have the pleasure of eating a big, fat, roast chicken then you must experience the pain involved in killing that self-same chicken. Gill and I squared this circle way back simply by giving up meat. We are not vegetarians – because we still eat eggs and fish – we just don't bother with the meat.

Shoestring hens

If you really want to get your chickens for little or no cost, then you could take on some ex-battery hens. In our area, the battery-hen people are quite happy to give us as many Rhode Island Red/Sussex cross hens as we can take. They are 40–59 weeks old and there is a high mortality rate, but they are completely free for the asking, and there is a lot of pleasure to be had in introducing them to the great outdoors.

Housing

It is best to get as big a chicken house as you can. We made ours from an old shed and a heap of salvaged wood. It measures about 3 m (10 ft) long and 2.4 m (8 ft) wide, and stands about 2.1 m (7 ft) high at the gutter line. The door is wide enough for a wheelbarrow, there is a sliding hatch-type window, a sliding hatch-type door for the chickens, and a range of nesting boxes that can be opened from outside. We can let the chickens in and out simply by pulling a rope, collect the eggs from the outside, and walk a barrow into the shed and clean the floor without lots of bending and backache. Our chicken house is ringed with a wire fence and a gate. We avoid most fox problems by locking the chickens in at night. The best way forward is to look at your plot, decide just how many chickens you want to keep, and then make the chicken house to suit.

Feeding

Much depends upon where you live. My son feeds his hens with a mix of boiled potato peelings from a local nursery school, his own kitchen waste, all the waste stuff from his vegetable garden, plus commercial chicken feed.

CHICKEN HOUSE MADE FROM AN OLD SHED

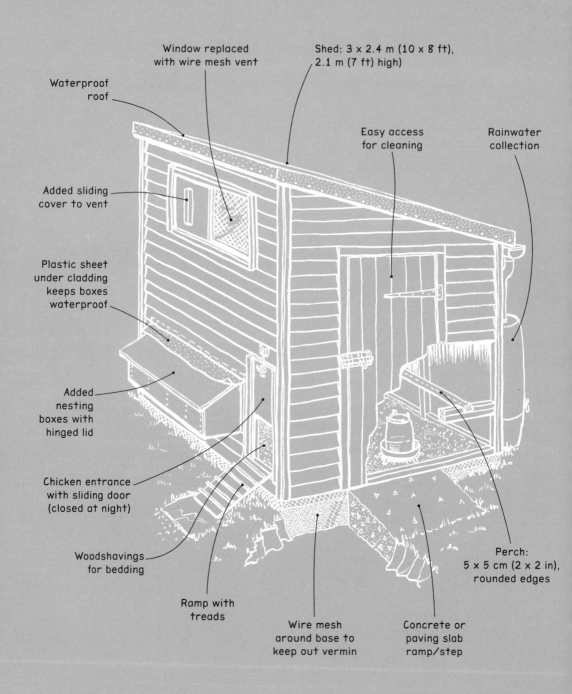

Waterproof roof

Window replaced with wire mesh vent

Shed: 3 x 2.4 m (10 x 8 ft), 2.1 m (7 ft) high

Easy access for cleaning

Rainwater collection

Added sliding cover to vent

Plastic sheet under cladding keeps boxes waterproof

Added nesting boxes with hinged lid

Chicken entrance with sliding door (closed at night)

Woodshavings for bedding

Ramp with treads

Wire mesh around base to keep out vermin

Concrete or paving slab ramp/step

Perch: 5 x 5 cm (2 x 2 in), rounded edges

CONSTRUCTION DETAILS FOR NESTING BOX AND VENT

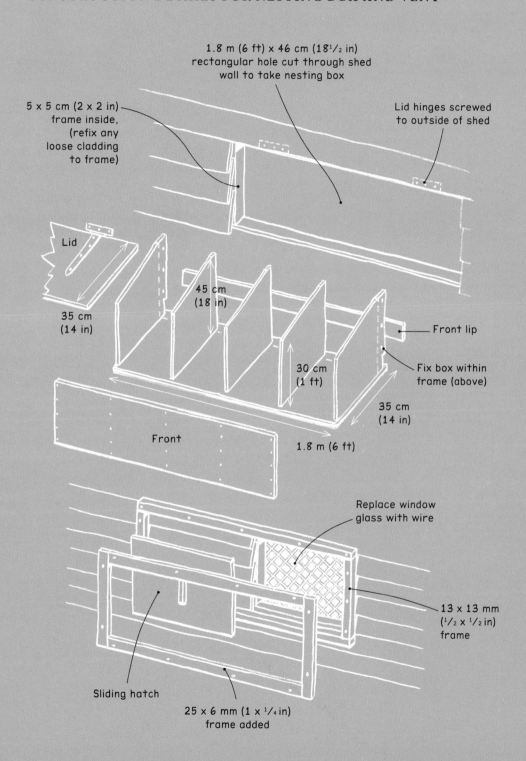

1.8 m (6 ft) x 46 cm (18¹/₂ in) rectangular hole cut through shed wall to take nesting box

5 x 5 cm (2 x 2 in) frame inside, (refix any loose cladding to frame)

Lid hinges screwed to outside of shed

Lid

35 cm (14 in)

45 cm (18 in)

30 cm (1 ft)

Front lip

Fix box within frame (above)

35 cm (14 in)

Front

1.8 m (6 ft)

Replace window glass with wire

13 x 13 mm (¹/₂ x ¹/₂ in) frame

Sliding hatch

25 x 6 mm (1 x ¹/₄ in) frame added

KEEPING PIGS

The way it was

In the 1970s, a friend kept pigs in the small field alongside his garden. He fed them on a mix of grain, milk from local farmers, and scraps from the school. When the pigs were the correct size, they were slaughtered in the local abattoir. He then gave choice joints to the various folk who had helped him, and the rest he salted down for bacon. The whole operation was controlled with little or no money changing hands.

Pigs and shoestring self-sufficiency

Keeping pigs only makes sense if you live in the country, are a meat eater, and have a by-product from some other activity. For example, it would work well if you had a house cow that gave more milk than you needed, and a good-sized vegetable plot that produced more than you could eat.

What you need to know

If you want pigs for little or no cost, get young pigs that are ready to leave their mother (you could barter for them). A pig needs a strong shelter to keep off the wind, sun, and rain, plenty of space, water on demand, and three feeds a day (as much as they can eat in 20 minutes). If they have some sort of free range for foraging, even better. Pigs are happiest in groups, like living out of doors, and need strong fencing to keep them in. In many countries there are now very strict health and safety regulations that govern how pigs are housed, fed, and slaughtered, and you must check these out for your area.

KEEPING GOATS

When our first child in arms developed a wheezy croak and our aged old lady neighbor told us that the best cure was goat's milk, we simply went to the livestock market and got ourselves a goat in milk. From then on, the whole business of keeping goats was a minefield of runaway goats and milking. And yes... the goat's milk remedy worked.

If you want to keep goats for milk, you must be aware that they are a 24/7 item. A good starter option is to get a female with her newborn kid in tow. This allows you to get the milk and to learn slowly about goats.

If you want lots of milk, make sure that you get the best goat that you can afford. A female with her kid needs a shed about 2.4–3 m (8–10 ft) square with some sort of lean-to at one side for the milking and food storage. They need plenty of food such as oats or maize, a daily feed of hay in winter, as much scrubland foraging as possible, and a constant supply of water.

Milking
We milked our goats twice a day – at sunrise and sunset. To do this, stand the goat on a wooden platform at a comfortable working height, clip her collar to a ring in the wall, wash her udders with warm water, and then milk her with a gentle, thumb-and-finger encircling, downward-stroking movement. If the goat kicks, loop the offending leg with a strap and hitch it up to one side.

VEGETARIAN MEALS FROM THE GARDEN

As I write, it is mid-summer and we have just been down to our vegetable plot to pick plums, courgettes (zucchini), beetroot, runner beans, broad beans, lettuces, radishes, cucumbers, and giant garlic. If we have a glut, we simply store it away for the winter or swap it. Currently, in exchange for our produce we have been getting duck eggs, stale bread for the geese, freshly made cakes from a neighbor, large cans of olive oil, logs for winter, and general help around the garden. It is a great time of the year – every day is slow and easy, eating the most beautiful fresh fruit and vegetables. We take turns doing the cooking. Yesterday Gill did a huge salad tossed in olive oil with sliced hard-boiled eggs, topped off with homemade chutney, with a slice of bread and honey to follow. Today I plan to do stir-fried courgettes (zucchini) with garlic bread on the side, washed down with last year's cider. We hope you enjoy the following recipes – they aren't fancy but they are amazingly low in cost and incredibly tongue-tinglingly tasty.

Courgettes (zucchini) with garlic toast

This is one of my favorites. It is swift and easy, it tastes absolutely scrumptious, it draws inspiration from the meals that my grandfather used to make, and I can make it a bit more special by adding tomatoes or a sprinkling of fresh fried plaice or goat's cheese.

* Onions
* Olive oil
* Freshly pulled garlic
* Small freshly picked courgettes (zucchini) – yellow or green
* Fresh brown bread – 2 thick slices per person
* Salted butter
* Freshly picked salad of choice
* Dry cider

Slice the onions thinly, and swiftly fry them in the olive oil. Crush the garlic, remove the skin, and finely chop the flesh. Slice and dice the courgettes (zucchini) and fry them with the onions. Toast the slices of brown bread and spread them with a thin layer of butter. To serve, top the toast with the fried onions and courgettes, sprinkle with the garlic, and dish up with the salad and a large glass of cold dry cider.

Gill's special summer salad

This is an ever-changing, beautiful meal – ever-changing because the precise ingredients will always have to be adjusted to suit whatever is currently in the garden.

* Land cress and salad leaves of choice
* Young carrots
* Onions
* Garlic
* Newly laid chicken eggs – 1½ per person
* Olive oil
* Chutney
* Fresh brown bread
* Salted butter

Swiftly wash and dry the land cress and salad leaves. Wash the carrots and slice them into long thin strips. Slice the onions. Crush the garlic and chop it into small lumps. Hard-boil the eggs. Put the leaves, carrots, onions, and garlic into a large bowl and turn them over with a generous amount of oil. Season to taste. Top the heap with the halved eggs, and serve with the chutney and buttered bread.

Stuffed marrow roast

This is a bit of a special meal for Sundays or when we have friends round. It takes a bit of time, but it is well worth the effort.

* One large marrow
* Onions
* Stale brown bread, grated
* Herbs of your choice – I like sage
* Olive oil
* New potatoes
* Salad leaves of your choice

Wash the marrow and slice and scoop out the inside, so that you finish up with a sort of long, lidded boat. Fry the onions and grated brown bread. Combine the fried mixture with the herbs and stuff the mixture into the marrow. Wipe the outside of the marrow over with olive oil. Wash the new potatoes but leave the skins in place. Oil the potatoes and pop them in the oven in the same dish as the stuffed marrow. Cook slowly at a medium temperature until the marrow is soft to the touch and the potatoes are firm-cooked and slightly leathery to the touch. Dish the marrow up as a centerpiece ringed with the potatoes, with the salad on the side.

Jess and Joe's toad-in-the-hole

This is a special meal for finger-licking kids – meaning children who really like to get in there and eat food with their fingers.

* Mugful of plain brown flour
* Mugful of fresh milk
* 2 fresh eggs
* Onions
* Courgettes (zucchini)
* Tomatoes
* Greek halloumi cheese
* Olive oil
* Herbs of choice

Beat the flour, milk, and eggs together to make a thick batter. Fry the chopped onions in the olive oil. Wash and chop the other vegetables and swiftly part-fry them alongside the onions. Spread the ingredients, together with thick slices of halloumi cheese, over the bottom of a thin-sided oven tray, drizzle with olive oil, add the herbs, and place in a hot oven. When the tray is hot, pour the batter over the ingredients and put into the oven for about 30 minutes until the mix is crisp and brown. Cut into huge slices and serve with homemade sauce or chutney.

WINTER MEALS
FROM THE GARDEN

Every other day throughout the cropping season we spend time squirreling away our garden produce. Harvest time is a wonderfully rewarding time of the year – it makes all the work and effort worthwhile. Gill carrying baskets of beans up from the garden, me trying to pick the biggest, best, and highest apples, swapping produce with neighbors, both of us heaving great wheelbarrow loads of courgettes (zucchini), stringing up onions – it is so good and so exciting. And, best of all, in between our harvesting sessions, when the sun is too hot for us to work, we just take a wedge of bread and cheese, creep off into the long grass, and have a picnic. It is amazing fun, after a couple hours spent gathering in the harvest, to do nothing more than just sit, eat, and laze about in the great outdoors.

Back in the house we salt beans and make chutneys and jams. We pickle things like onions, beetroots, walnuts, and courgettes (zucchini), we dry-hang onions and garlic, we freeze fruits like raspberries, plums, strawberries, and apple pulp, we freeze runner beans and broad beans, we freeze part-cooked messes made from onions, peppers, courgettes, and aubergines (eggplants), and we freeze items like eggs, fish, and rabbit. Of course, these storing sessions are a bit tedious and most definitely hard work and sweat-making, but when winter comes around it is a real treat to be able to take prepared food from our stores. The following recipes will give you a taste of what we are all about.

Onion, garlic, and potato soup with goat's cheese

This soup is great, especially when you have a cold or flu. If you are in any way congested or under the weather, then this is the meal to go for. It is swift and easy to make and it tastes all the better for keeping.

* Onions – taken from your dry-hang store
* Garlic – taken from your dry-hang store
* Potatoes
* Olive oil – best quality
* Salted butter
* Fresh brown bread – best if it is warm and crusty
* Salted butter
* Hard goat's cheese

Slice the onions and swiftly fry them in a large pan with the olive oil. Crush the garlic, remove the skin and add to the onions. Boil the potatoes, strain them, and add them to the onion and garlic mix. Three-quarters fill the pan with water and gently simmer until the potatoes break down. To serve, spoon the soup into large bowls and dish up with torn lumps of buttered brown bread and chunks of cheese.

Alan's rabbit shepherd's pie

As vegetarians, this is a meal that we cook for our meat-eating friends. We shoot our own rabbits, but you could just as well use squirrel, pigeons, or perhaps some sort of shop-bought gamey meat.

* Rabbit or game of your choice
* Flour
* Olive oil
* Potatoes
* Carrots
* Peas
* Runner beans
* Tinned or bottled tomatoes
* Onions
* Salted butter

Skin and gut the rabbit and very carefully cut it down into joints. Roll the joints in flour and swiftly flash-fry them in the olive oil in a large pan. Add water to the pan and boil and simmer the joints until the flesh falls from the bones. Remove all the bones. Boil the potatoes and the carrots. Mash the potatoes. Strain off the ingredients and layer them in a large deep oven pan/dish: carrots, peas, beans, tomatoes, onions, and rabbit, carrots, peas, beans, tomatoes, onions, and rabbit, and so on – until you get to within an inch or so of the top of the dish. Pour some of the rabbit stock over the layers and top it all off with a generous layer of mashed potatoes. Finally smear butter over the potatoes and slow cook in a medium hot oven.

Alan and Gill's courgette (zucchini), onion, tomato, and aubergine (eggplant) pot roast

During the summer we make and freeze what we call our 'messes.' To make a mess, we cut and dice onions, courgettes (zucchini), tomatoes, and aubergines (eggplants), swiftly flash-fry them – two portions at a time – in olive oil and then put the resultant mix in plastic bags in the freezer. We aim to make about 10 two-person portions at a session. Although we use such a mess in this recipe, you can make the meal from starters, as described below. This is one of those meals that we keep going for the best part of a week. We usually have a meal, add extra carrots, have another meal, pop in some dumplings, and so on. It all adds up to lots of beautiful winter meals.

* Onions
* Carrots
* Courgettes (zucchini)
* Tomatoes
* Aubergines (eggplants)
* Potatoes
* Broad beans
* Herbs of your choice
* Olive oil

Wash and dice the onions, carrots, courgettes (zucchini), tomatoes, aubergines (eggplants), and potatoes. Flash-fry these in olive oil in a large pan. When the mix is nicely browned and sealed, add water, the broad beans, and herbs to taste, bring to the boil and gently simmer. Serve with brown bread on the side.

MAKING CHUTNEY

Chutney and self-reliance

The taste and texture of chutney is a foodie evocation of the make-do-and-mend spirit; it speaks of warm beer, pub lunches, the smell of fruit, rural traditions, and of course self-reliant shoestring living. The very notion of chutney has to do with making the best of what you have. One moment you have a glut of over-ripe apples, great heaps of onions that are too small or misshapen to keep, lots of under-ripe green tomatoes that need picking, and all manner of odds and ends of vegetables that you really don't know what to do with, and the next you have a delicious brown pickle or preserve that is completely different in taste and texture from its component parts.

Chutney recipes

When I was a child, every mum, granny, aunt, daughter, and sister had their own unique chutney recipe. The method is simple. You simmer the ingredients – items like tomatoes, apples, onions, garlic, runner beans, dates, and sultanas – with just enough vinegar to cover. Then add sugar, herbs, and spices to the mix, continue simmering, and store the resultant brown mixture in airtight jars. The wonderful thing about chutney is the fact that the basic recipe can be adjusted ad infinitum to suit individual needs and tastes. For example, I like apples, onions, garlic, carrots, and beans, and particularly dislike sultanas and dates, so I simply replace the latter with things that I do like.

MAKING JAM

Jam and the good life

When the queen in Lewis Carroll's *Through The Looking Glass* said 'The rule is, jam tomorrow and jam yesterday – but never jam today,' she was describing a pleasure that was so exceptional that it could never be realized. It was a promise of good things that would never come. In our shoestring paradise, however, it is possible for you to have the very best food that you could ever wish to eat, plus 'jam on it'.

Jam on everything

In the context of this book, jam is defined as mashed fruit that has been boiled with sugar and water, while jelly is much the same product but with all the seeds and pulp removed. The method is simple. You just simmer the prepared fruit or vegetable – plums, apples, raspberries, strawberries, red-, white-, or blackcurrants, gooseberries, blackberries, oranges, rhubarb, peaches, or just about any fruit that grows in your area – with a little water, add sugar to the mix, continue simmering until the mix starts to thicken and set, and then store the brightly colored, semi-jellied spread in airtight jars. If you have only tasted shop-bought jam, the taste and smell of homemade jam is so intense that it is almost beyond description. Jam making completely changes the character of the fruit being preserved, to the extent that it becomes a different product in its own right.

Blackberry jam

* 1.8 kg (4 lb) blackberries
* 1.7 liters (3 pints) water
* 2.7 kg (6 lb) sugar

Method
1 Remove the blackberry stalks and put the fruit into a preserving pan with the water.
2 Simmer gently until the fruit is tender and the contents of the pan are reduced – this takes about 45 minutes.
3 Add the sugar, stir, and boil rapidly for 10–15 minutes until the mixture starts to set.
4 Pour the jam into warm jars.

Marrow jam

* 1.8 kg (4 lb) marrow, peeled
* 1.6 kg (3½ lb) sugar
* Juice of 2 lemons
* Rind of ½ lemon
* 60 g (2 oz) root ginger

Method
1 Remove the seed and pulp of the marrow, cut into small pieces, and steam until tender.
2 Place in a pan, cover with the sugar, add the lemon juice and rind, and leave overnight.
3 Put the contents into a preserving pan, and add the root ginger tied in muslin.
4 Cook until thick and syrupy – this takes about an hour.
5 Remove the ginger and pour the jam into warm jars.

POWER

SHOESTRING INSULATION

In the 1970s, when Gill and I started out on the self-sufficiency road, the primary concern when it came to heating a home was how to save energy by increasing the insulation. The best that we could come up with at that time – because we were short of money and desperately trying to make ends meet – was to increase the insulation in the roof space, walls, and floor cavities, to have double glazing, to hang thick, heavy curtains at the windows and doors, to have sausage-shaped, rag-stuffed draught excluders at every door, to have a sort of air-lock porch at both outside doors, and generally to wear more clothes to suit the outside temperatures. And it really does work.

Insulation materials

Have a look in your roof space, and if the insulation is any thinner than 15 cm (6 in) then you need more. Perhaps the best way forward is to take advantage of any government grants and simply to increase the insulation. By far the cheapest form of roof insulation is fiberglass; however, it is a very unpleasant material to work with and carries some health concerns. Some eco options that are worth saving up for include cellulose (newspaper, cardboard, cotton, straw, sawdust), sheep's wool, or shredded waste fabric.

SHOESTRING PHOTOVOLTAIC PANELS

When Gill and I started out, photovoltaic (PV) energy was no more than an offshoot of the space industry that was just beginning to be used to power things like boats, caravans, and remote research stations. In 1970 a single solar panel would have cost me about six months' salary. Now, of course, PVs are everywhere – on roofs as panels and tiles, built into the structure of buildings, and even in some instances built into the very glass that makes up the windows. The blue-black cells are most generally seen as electrically connected arrays packaged within glass frames. The solar panels produce electricity directly from sunlight. Research suggests that photovoltaics are most definitely the future.

Advantages
* Sunlight is plentiful
* Solar power is pollution-free during use.
* PV installations can operate for many years with minimum maintenance
* There are no moving parts to be serviced
* Solar electrics can be used for remote off-grid situations
* Solar electric generation can be used to replace grid electricity
* Grid-connected solar electricity can be used locally

Disadvantages

* Solar electricity is more expensive than most other forms of small-scale alternative energy production
* Solar PV panels are less affordable than say solar hot water or solar space heating
* Solar electricity is not produced at night and is greatly reduced in cloudy conditions
* Solar cells produce direct current (DC) electricity which must be converted to alternating current (AC)

Buying photovoltaics on a shoestring

Although you can in many countries buy into various government schemes that allow you to pay off the costs over say a period of 20 years, these schemes are difficult to understand and ponderous to navigate. We looked at the paperwork and decided that the workings of the scheme were beyond our understanding. After a lot of research, we decided to buy our panels directly from China. The following diary account will give you some idea of the procedure.

Diary of events

* Spent a day searching on the internet. After a lot of difficulties, I managed – through an intermediary company – to send an email directly through to a Chinese company.
* Have just received an email written in broken English from a Chinese guy called 'George Angel.'
* Have sent an email telling George our needs – I said we wanted a 3 kW system for an off-grid situation.
* George has sent me an email listing his company's products – I see that I can buy individual panels or a whole system in kit form. It appears that I will need the panels, an inverter, lots of cables and connections, and a bank of batteries.
* We have decided to buy a 3 kW kit complete with everything bar the batteries. I have asked George to send us details and costs.
* Have received the order form and paperwork. George now needs the address of our nearest seaport.
* Went to the bank with the paperwork and transferred funds directly through to the Chinese company. It wasn't easy.
* Have received an email from George. He has received our money and has given us a delivery date – should arrive in 6–8 weeks' time. Today I purchased a bank of ten batteries online.

* Have just received a phone call from an import-export company saying that our goods have arrived at the port of destination. We need to pay the import duty and various charges and we need to organize transport – all has to be done fast!
* We visited the docks in a rented truck and collected the goods in person. Everything was fraught with difficulties – getting onto the docks, getting the goods through customs, getting away.
* The system is beautiful – really good quality.

Conclusion

The various import taxes and duties doubled the initial cost. The system itself cost $1,600/£1000, but the total cost was $3,200/£2000. I see that the same Chinese system bought directly from a local supplier in this country would have cost us approximately $19,200/£12,000 fitted, so we have saved about $16,000/£10,000, but of course we still have to do the fitting.

SOLAR WATER HEATERS

A solar water heater is a beautifully elegant system. Cold water goes in, the sun shines, and hot water comes out. The more sun, the hotter the water. Although over the years we have built various DIY systems, experience tells me that the best shoestring way forward is not to build one, but to get the very best commercial system at the lowest possible price. If you are looking for something really special, then go for Microsolar.

Advantages
* Sunlight is plentiful
* Solar power is pollution free during use
* Solar water systems can operate for many years with minimum maintenance
* Apart from a few valves and taps, there are no moving parts to be serviced
* Solar water heaters can be used for remote off-grid situations

Disadvantages
* Solar electricity is not produced at night and is greatly reduced in cloudy conditions
* Solar systems need a back-up for cloudy days

Buying a solar hot water system on a shoestring

Most solar hot water collectors are made in places like China and Malaysia. When we researched buying in the UK, we swiftly learnt that local companies put their logos on Chinese items and then put huge mark-ups on the end costs. We came to the conclusion that our best way forward was to buy direct from a Chinese or Malaysian company.

Diary of events

* Spent a whole day searching on the internet. I see that one of the best companies – Microsolar – operates from Selangor in Malaysia.
* I have made contact via email with a certain Mr Siang Teoh – the founder owner of the Microsolar company. His credentials and background are amazing: prizewinning architectural student educated in Scotland, winner of all sorts of prestigious prizes, designer and builder of solar schemes in Nepal, and so on. Suffice to say that Siang Teoh is the right man.
* We have agreed a price with Siang Teoh for three 360-liter coaxial Multivalve Thermosyphon Solar Water Heaters. I will give one system to my eldest son.
* Went to the bank and sent the money through – all swift and easy.
* Had email confirmation that all is correct – the goods are on their way.
* We hired a huge truck plus a driver and went to the docks. The package was huge – all together in a single container. The import company craned the crate onto the back of the lorry. When we got back to the house, we cut the various containers apart so that they could be handled by two people.
* We have built a huge wooden 'A' on a flat roof – large enough to take two 360-liter systems – see the photographs.
* Fitting and plumbing was easy. The rising cold water mains water goes in one end and the hot water comes out the other. We have fitted a small electric heater on the delivery side to give the water a boost on cold and cloudy days.

Conclusion

About two years later the systems are still running perfectly. One day's sun gives us enough hot water for around three days. Even in icy weather, as long as the sun is shining, they deliver. Last year in winter we had a major freeze-up. In a panic I emailed Siang Teoh and he was wonderfully helpful. I see that since we made contact with Microsolar all sorts of Chinese 'clone' companies have sprung up with company names that link Micro and Solar. Be warned – you need to make contact with the original Microsolar Company.

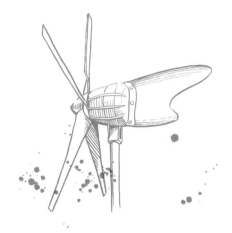

SHOESTRING
WIND TURBINES

The first thing we did when we got started with self-sufficiency in the mid-1970s was to build our own wind turbine. It was the thing to do. If you were going to be self-sufficient or in any way be involved in the good life, you just had to build a wind turbine. Although at that time – really before computers – there were very few commercial turbines on the market, there were all sorts of articles in magazines and counterculture handouts that told you how to make your own turbines from bits of car or bicycle, with hand-carved prop blades. As I saw it, making a small turbine to light a single 12-volt bulb was one thing, but making one large enough to power a whole house was quite another. Remember that at that time wind turbines were thought to be futuristic and iconic, like something out of 'Star Trek.'

Having written to various communes across America and made contact with Stewart Brand, publisher of *The Whole Earth Catalog* (the American counterculture catalog), we decided to go big and build one using bits and pieces from a lorry. I will not bore you with all the construction details but, when the great day came for the big launch, the wind blew, we threw the switch, our lights flashed, the wiring sizzled and burst into flames, and the whole rotor head came adrift and cartwheeled across the meadow. It was a glorious disaster.

The trouble with wind turbines

Although over the years we have experimented with wind turbines (both making and importing them), I have got to say that so many machines are now coming on to the market – big ones from China, small ones, micro ones, ones with self-supporting towers, ones that fit flat against a wall, and so on – that the whole subject of wind turbines has become somewhat muddy and confused. While I would have said five or so years ago that a medium-sized 3 kW machine is the one to go for (indeed we helped purchase one for a friend), our experiences with that particular machine and machines of the same ilk have been so fraught with problems – inverter failure, trouble in high winds, and nothing but complaints from distraught neighbors – that really we have lost confidence in wind turbines. For example, having purchased a small 2 kW turbine to sell on to a guy who has a smallholding in Spain, he now tells us that while they are wonderful when they are working they take countless hours of nursing and servicing.

Conclusion – the way to go

To recap, having been thinking and working with wind turbines for half a lifetime, I am now of the opinion that the current development is so fast, furious, highly competitive, and ongoing that really the best advice if you are committed to shoestring self-sufficiency is to play around and experiment with small DIY machines made from bicycle parts or similar, but also to keep one eye on the research and development of micro turbines. My gut feeling, when it comes down to turbines designed to power say a family house, is that the future is going to be in micro turbines. Research suggests that we are fast approaching a time when, rather than having say one large 3 kW turbine per house, we will all be having arrays of 50 or so micro turbines, with each little turbine pushing out a few watts. I think that in the context of domestic wind turbines size does matter, and in this instance it will be small that is beautiful.

PASSIVE SOLAR GAIN

Traditionally, in pre-industrial times, houses were placed so that they took best advantage of water supplies, roads, tracks, the shape of the landscape, and passive direct solar gain. If your homesteading or pioneering great-great-grandfather had the choice and was able to construct his own house, he would have walked around his land, taken note of the direction of the sun at midday, the position of trees, hills, mountains, and anything else that might have impacted on his comfort and well-being, and then set about building the house accordingly. He would have organized room design and usage so that the sun shone in his bedroom at sunrise and followed him around the house. If he got it right, the sun would still be shining on him at the end of the day when he was having his supper. Of course the back of the house would also be sheltered from prevailing wind and weather. He would have done all this by copying what his parents had done before him and by instinct. Now of course, when builders drop houses down on a plot willy-nilly with small regard to anything other than profit, the problem we have is how to modify our houses so that they take best advantage of the sun.

Passive solar gain

In a passive solar house, everything about the building – its shape, size, and structure and all the windows, walls, and floors – is designed to collect, store, or in some way use solar energy. Ideally, all this is done passively without the use of any electromechanical systems. A common example is a solarium on the side of a building that faces the sun at midday. Another example is a window high in the roof that cools the house by allowing hot air to rise. Passive solar technologies include direct and indirect solar gain for space heating, the use of thermal mass for reducing indoor air temperature swings, and the solar chimney for natural ventilation. The ultimate solar house would use mirrored surfaces to direct sunlight through the house, matt black surfaces for absorbing heat, shades for cooling, surfaces to absorb and radiate heat, green roofs to cut down the heat in high summer, double glazing, insulation, and so on.

What we did with our house
* The first thing that we did with our little wooden cottage was to walk around it and see how it sat with the sun.
* We replaced all the windows with double glazing.
* We put a porch on the back door to cut down on winter draughts.
* We packed high-quality natural hemp insulation into the walls and roof space – the rooms are now warm in winter and cool in summer.
* We built a long, low solarium or conservatory along the side of the house that faced the sun at midday.
* We fitted a stable door to the solarium.
* We put a solar water heater on the roof.
* We fitted the solarium with thermal mass structures to hold the heat: brick floors, brick raised beds full of dark-colored crushed stone, and various smaller brick structures.
* We fitted simple vents into the house walls and solarium walls so that we can control ventilation and direct stored heat through the house.

Conclusion
The solarium is truly wonderful, especially in spring and autumn because it seems to shorten the winter. The brick structures warm up slowly throughout the day and then just as slowly give out heat. The vents – at floor and ceiling level in both the house and the solarium – allow us variously to direct hot air into the house, draw cool air from the house into the solarium, and draw cool air through the solarium and on through the house. The stable door allows us to direct cool air through to the house.

Although many of these changes might seem to be minimal, low cost, and altogether too easy, the fact is that they make a huge difference to our comfort. For example, having breakfast in the solarium on an early spring morning – when the weather outside is cold, blustery, and otherwise unpleasant – is a simple but wonderful pleasure.

LIFESTYLE

WORKING FROM HOME

Thinking it through

If you are considering full-time self-sufficiency, the first thing is to figure out how you are going to make the money to pay for things like property rates/tax, fuel for the car, and clothes. You need to sit down with a pen and paper and do the sums. Ask yourself some questions. Do you plan to do part-time local work in a shop or some sort of industry? Do you have a money-making art or craft activity? Will you create a saleable product such as meat, fruit, vegetables, honey, or eggs? As part of the equation, you need to take into account that any activity that requires you to dress up in smart clothes and drive off in a car does in itself cost money.

How we do it

When we first started out, I worked as a lecturer in a local college while Gill stayed at home with the kids and did a small amount of craftwork. It partly worked because of my long summer holidays, but at the same time it was frustrating because we could not make any headway with our crafts and self-sufficiency activities. We eventually reached a point where we had to bite the bullet and give up the teaching work. Although we were then doing our craftwork full time – Gill doing woven textiles and me doing pottery – we soon realized that we were going to run out of money. To cut a long, and sometimes painful, story short, we started writing for craft magazines, and then we did a mix of writing and illustration, and so on until we had enough money to get by. That said, we have always had to make choices and compromises. For example, what is Gill doing at this moment when she would prefer to be outside in the vegetable garden? She is sitting at her desk doing illustrations. The good news is that we can, if we choose, do deskwork when it is raining, or at least try to do it in the winter. We can, to a great extent, shape our activities to suit our needs and fancies. The other interesting thing is that gradually over the years we have made money from what we think of as our pleasure activities. For example, my interest in tractors and wind turbines has brought in money, Gill's spinning skills have brought in money – all these little bits of money help to make the whole thing work. To recap, we earn cash from our writing and illustration work, we grow our own food, we sell produce at the gate, and we make money from our various pleasure activities.

Computers and the internet

Although not so long ago working from home usually involved some sort of cottage industry – bringing in or producing basic raw materials, making a product, and selling it at the gate or at a local outlet – the coming of the computer and the internet has changed all that. For example, we know many people who live in places as far apart as South America and India who use their computers in end-of-garden sheds to make their self-sufficiency lifestyle possible. One designs books, another works part-time for a company that allows him to do his work from home, another is an editor, another buys and sells wind turbines, and so on. Our computers and the internet allow us to make contact with people all over the world, see each other at the flick of a switch, do research, and sell and buy goods – the possibilities are endless.

TRADING AND GIFTING

Currently we grow fruit and vegetables, and keep geese for eggs and bees for honey. Although initially, when we planned our set-up, we thought that all of this produce would be for our own use, we are finding that we have surplus vegetables, eggs, and honey. Offering this surplus for sale brings us into contact with people who would much prefer to gift and exchange goods and services than deal with cash.

For example, a man who came to buy our eggs offered to mend my tractor in exchange for the eggs. A neighbor cooks us a cake and gives it to us in return for us occasionally doing a bit of market shopping. When the man who sells us logs wanted our wind turbine expertise, we came to a very loose and informal agreement where he gives us logs in exchange for our know-how.

It is something of a surprise to us, but gradually over the last five years or so we have found that when it comes to fencing, our tractor, surplus honey, eggs, and vegetables, the occasional beautiful home-baked cake, logs for heating, and our know-how we have become involved in a sort of 'gift economy' – which the dictionary defines as 'a society where goods or services are given for other goods or services without using a medium of exchange, such as money, and without there being a formal understanding that future rewards will be received.'

**WE ARE NOT TO THROW AWAY THOSE
THINGS THAT BENEFIT OUR NEIGHBOR.
GOODS ARE CALLED GOOD BECAUSE
THEY CAN BE USED FOR GOOD: THEY ARE
INSTRUMENTS FOR GOOD, IN THE HANDS
OF THOSE WHO USE THEM PROPERLY.**

CLEMENT OF ALEXANDRIA (C. 150–215)

REDUCE,
REUSE, RECYCLE

When in the late 1960s NASA released the first satellite photo of the sphere Earth as seen from space, and we all saw with own eyes that everything – all our homes, family, friends, food, forests, animals, rivers, seas – is down here on Earth, we were not alone in feeling frightened and uneasy. Our planet looked so fragile and alone. Then the questions started to be asked. Why is it that we were making such a mess of our planet? If it is so fragile and unique, why are we treating it like a vast toilet?

So here we are, half a lifetime later, and the people in power are still pushing the message that the only way to get out of this mess is, as a consumer society, to consume more – or squander, waste, destroy, use up, and expend. The good news is that most of us realize that even at a very basic level recycling saves money and resources, reduces pollution, and creates jobs. The bad news is that most of us – countries, governments, industries, towns, villages, you, me, and the person next door – still do next to nothing.

**USE IT UP, WEAR IT OUT,
MAKE IT DO, OR DO WITHOUT.**

NEW ENGLAND PROVERB

RECLAIMED MATERIALS AND THEIR USES

Aluminum
* At one time aluminum was more valuable than gold
* We have used aluminum sheet to mend a shed floor and make various covers and structures
* Recycling plants welcome aluminum

Batteries
* Batteries contain harmful metal and toxic fluids
* We use them for small tasks and then recycle them
* Take them to your local recycling center

Brick
* A good brick is virtually indestructible – and is a beautiful item
* We have used recycled bricks for paths, floors, decorative details around the house and garden, and as rubble
* Bricks are always useful – keep them

Concrete
* Concrete is an environmentally expensive material
* We use smashed-up concrete as hardcore in our various foundations
* You could hire a small crushing machine and reuse the concrete as dry aggregate

Copper
* Copper is a mineral that is found in the Earth's crust – recycling copper saves energy
* We save our waste copper from pipes and electrical wiring, and sell it on
* You could sell it on or turn it into decorative items

Electrical equipment
* Electrical items variously contain gold, silver, copper, lead, and mercury
* We mend items, use them as far as we can, and then try to sell on
* You could do as we do or take them to the local recycling center

Furniture
* Recycling furniture helps to divert many tonnes of waste from landfills
* As woodworkers, we rework and mend our furniture – it is a fun activity
* You could give it to a recycling organization or give it a makeover

Glass
* Most glass can be easily recycled
* Reuse jars and bottles for sauce, chutney, and jam making – and send the rest to a recycling center
* In some countries, it is possible to make money by recycling glass

Mobiles
* One mobile phone was found to contain gold, silver, copper, palladium, and platinum
* We hold on to our phones until they literally wear thin – we then sell them to a recycler
* Almost every part of the phone can be recycled or sold

Paint
* Unused paint is one of the most avoidable household hazard waste materials
* We use up all the odds and ends to paint our sheds – the door red, one side yellow, a panel red, etc
* You can give left-over paint to charities and high school drama groups

Oil
* Discarded oil can end up in landfills, drains, and water systems – in the West improper disposal is a crime
* We don't use much oil, but I use my left-overs to oil the tractor
* You can do as we do or take it to a local recycling center

Paper
* 90% of paper is made of wood – papermaking accounts for about one-third of felled trees
* We put most of our card and paper on the compost heap

Plastic
* The oceans contain vast amounts of plastic debris
* We use it for various projects and take the rest to the recycling center
* Do as we do – never put plastic in landfill

Steel
* Recycling steel saves huge amounts of iron ore and fossil fuel
* We recycle containers and use all posts, bars, and sheets to destruction
* Do as we do or sell it to a scrap metal merchant

Textiles
* Almost every part of a garment can be recycled
* We only buy natural fibers (cotton, wool, and linen), use them until they fall apart and then put them on the compost heap
* You can do as we do, or sell on to a recycling company

Vehicles
* At the end of the 19th century over half the cars were electric
* We use our cars to destruction and sell them on to a scrap yard – we also use parts of bicycles for carts, go-karts and small wind turbines
* Do as we do, or see how long you can keep your car on the road

Wood
* In some parts of America wood grows faster than it can be harvested
* We use all our wood to destruction, use it to mend sheds, structures, fences, and gates, and then finally put it on the compost heap
* Almost every piece of wood can be reworked or recycled – old wood makes good furniture

MAKE-DO-AND-MEND

In much the same way as Robinson Crusoe started by stripping his wrecked ship of rope, iron, fabrics, copper cable, and such like, and then building his world afresh using a mix of salvaged materials and whatever natural materials he could find on the island, Gill and I have created our self-sufficient world using a mix of natural materials and recycled waste. In and around our home, we have used old bricks for floors, salvaged doors and timbers for some of the interiors, salvaged metal and plastic containers in the vegetable garden, used bits of this and that for some of the fences and gates, salvaged timber and metal sheeting to make garden sheds and shelters, used offcuts and giveaways from timber yards for some of the decorative details, used old wheels to make garden carts, used bits salvaged from ships for lighting and windows, and so on. We have even made a wind turbine from old telegraph poles and old car parts.

Self-sufficiency on a shoestring is about looking at your life afresh. So, if some item in our home breaks or needs building – a coat hook, a shed, a table, a chair, a lamp – our first response is not to dip into our hard-earned money and buy a new product, but rather to look around and see if we can rework or make use of an existing item or material. Over the years we have discovered that the environment invariably somehow provides materials and solutions, but sometimes you do have to be patient. For example, you may want some insulation for a wall but will have to wait for the right material to come along – rest assured that it always will!

The saying or slogan 'make-do-and-mend' has its beginnings in the Second World War when fabric and materials were in such short supply that people were encouraged to mend and repair rather than buy new. My grandfather, an ex-navy man, was so skilled at make-do-and-mend that he could make just about anything from anything. For example, when I repeatedly said that I wanted a sheath knife, he took a leaf spring from an old car, built a little forge out of odds and ends of brick, wood, and leather, made charcoal from a pile of apple wood, and then simply made a knife. By the time he had finished hammering the blade, binding a handle with intricate knotwork, and cutting and sewing an old thick leather school bag to make the sheath, I had just about the biggest, best, sharpest, and fanciest knife in the village.

The strange, topsy-turvy, thing is that while my grandpa had no choice other than to make-do-and-mend, simply because he was poor and because before and after the wars manufactured materials were difficult to come by, Gill and I are now doing much the same thing because we live in a rich society that is awash with waste manufactured materials. Miraculously, by the time the war was over, people were so proud of their make-do-and-mend efforts and abilities that a repaired jacket, a scarf knitted from recycled wool, a pair of painstakingly repaired sandals, a go-kart made from an old pram, or indeed my knife, ceased being symbols of poverty and became instead badges of honour – each one a symbol that stood for pride in oneself, achievement, and creativity.

ONE LAST THOUGHT

For us, the wonderful thing about shoestring self-sufficiency is the way it allows us to give our creativity free reign. For example, when we built the interior of our old wooden house from recycled bricks and timber, the prime motivation was not to save money (although of course that was a factor) but simply to see if we could do it. When the house was finished, we enjoyed just sitting and remembering the various near-impossible physical tasks that we had achieved, such as the way we lifted massive timbers with pulleys and jacks, and how Gill, by means of a simple lever and steel rollers, was able to swing a heavy timber beam into place. We derive pleasure from knowing that, but for our creativity and physical efforts, the bricks and timber would be no more than heaps of materials.

So it is every day of the week. We delight in working out how we can solve tasks – mending the greenhouse, taking a piece of machinery to pieces, building another shed from waste materials, mending a tool, patching a piece of clothing, moving an item that looks to be immovable, and so on. These are all exciting, creative, and therapeutic challenges that should not be missed. For us at least, a large part of the fun is not so much in the end result but in the doing.

IT IS NOT WHAT YOU LOOK AT THAT MATTERS, IT IS WHAT YOU SEE.

HENRY DAVID THOREAU (1817–1862)

RESOURCES

Harrowsmith
A back-to-the-land environmental magazine geared to countryside rural living, founded in 1976. The very best editions range from 1976 through to 1988. Old copies are deeply informative.

www.direct.gov.uk/en/ environmentandgreenerliving
UK government recycling, energy saving, vegetable growing, keeping livestock and general eco site.

www.carboncalculator.direct.gov.uk
General CO_2 calculator.

www.energysavingtrust.org.uk
UK organization that gives advice on cutting energy and reducing carbon emissions.

www.defra.gov.uk
UK government site that sets out policies on the environment, food, and rural affairs.

www.countrysmallholding.com
The *Country Smallholding* magazine site which has lots of information on small-scale farming – livestock, fences, gates, sheds, etc.

www.epa.gov
US Environmental Protection Agency site that has lots of information on air pollution, drinking water, eCycling, farming, etc.

www.epa.gov/climatechange/kids
'A student's guide to global climate change', aimed at the lower age range.

http://globe.gov
The Global Learning and Observations to Benefit the Environment (GLOBE) – an education program for schools targeted at hands-on, primary and secondary school-based science and education.

http://gcmd.nasa.gov
NASA's Global Change Master Directory (GCMD) gives open access to information relevant to global change.

www.nrel.gov
National Renewable Energy Laboratory, US Department of Energy.

www.backwoodshome.com
The *Backwoods Home Magazine* site, which has practical ideas for self-reliant living.

www.livinggreenmag.com
Online magazine about sustainable choices for home, work, and community.

www.insulation4less.com
Provides lots of detailed information about house insulation.

www.decc.gov.uk
Department of Energy and Climate Change site.

www.jacobswind.net
Jacobs have been producing wind turbines since 1922 and are considered by many to be the best.

www.windturbine.net/products.htm
Jacobs wind systems – details, leads, and prices.

www.microsolarusa.com
Microsolar water heaters in the US – see sites for other countries and also 'direct from factory' sales. Thought by many to be the best in the field.

www.homesteadingtoday.com
Online forum and community of individuals who are getting 'back to the land', and general homesteading advice.

INDEX

Acknowledgements

Photographs: Alan and Gill Bridgewater (page 187), Fotolia and Photos.com (page 102).